SHORT BIKE RIDES™
IN MINNESOTA

Help Us Keep This Guide Up to Date

Every effort has been made by the author and editors to make this guide as accurate and useful as possible. However, many things can change after a guide is published—establishments close, phone numbers change, hiking trails are rerouted, facilities come under new management, and so forth.

We would love to hear from you concerning your experiences with this guide and how you feel it could be made better and be kept up to date. While we may not be able to respond to all comments and suggestions, we'll take them to heart, and we'll also make certain to share them with the author. Please send your comments and suggestions to the following address:

The Globe Pequot Press
Reader Response/Editorial Department
P.O. Box 833
Old Saybrook, CT 06475

Or you can e-mail us at:

editorial@globe-pequot.com

Thanks for your input, and happy travels!

Short Bike Rides™ Series

Short Bike Rides™ in Minnesota

By

Mark Weinberger

Old Saybrook, Connecticut

Cover photo: Chris Dubé
Cover design: Saralyn D'Amato-Twomey

Short Bike Rides is a trademark of The Globe Pequot Press.

Library of Congress Cataloging-in-Publication Data

Weinberger, Mark (Mark Robert)
 Short bike rides in Minnesota / by Mark Weinberger.—1st ed.
    p.   cm. — (Short bike rides series)
  ISBN 0-7627-0207-9
  1. Bicycle touring—Minnesota—Guidebooks. 2. Bicycle trails—
Minnesota—Guidebooks. 3. Minnesota—Guidebooks. I. Title. II. Series.
GV1045.5.M6W45   1998   97-45734
917.7604'53—dc21   CIP

♻ This book is printed on recycled paper.
Manufactured in the United States of America
First Edition/First Printing

For my parents, Robert Weinberger and
Lorraine Weinberger (1925–1989),
who kept me supplied with bikes,
supported all my endeavors,
and always encouraged without pushing.

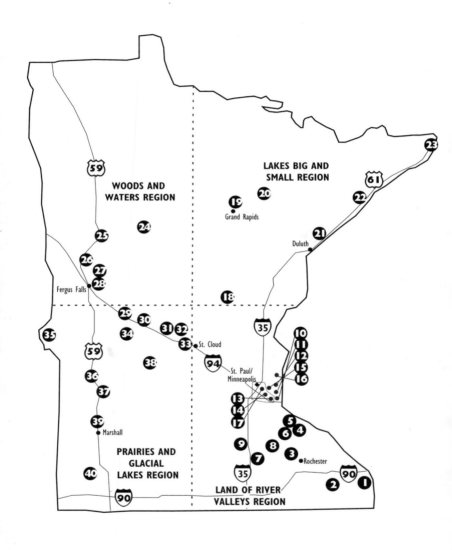

LAKES BIG AND SMALL REGION

WOODS AND WATERS REGION

Grand Rapids

Duluth

Fergus Falls

St. Cloud

St. Paul/ Minneapolis

Marshall

Rochester

PRAIRIES AND GLACIAL LAKES REGION

LAND OF RIVER VALLEYS REGION

Contents

Prairies and Glacial Lakes

Appendices

Acknowledgments

The cyclists listed below suggested routes, helped me ride and map them, and tolerated my many stops to record mileages and take pictures. Next time around I'll try to improve my bike-handling skills so I can do some of that work while still riding. Thanks to Henry Thomas (who usually took me away from my desk at least one day during the workweek), Mark Kieffer, Lynda Bergeson, Dave Asp, Joe Seeb, Henry Djerlev, Steve Stillwell, George Odio, and Noel Reider.

I also want to thank Cindi Pietrzyk, my editor, for the opportunity and encouragement throughout the process. And thanks to my cousin Ed Whitledge, who unknowingly helped with this project many years ago by running alongside me down the alley as I did one of my first rides on an adult bike. I did crash, but it did wonders for my balance in the long run. Thanks also to my brother Bruce for his enthusiastic support.

Finally, a heartfelt thanks to my wife, Lisa, who traveled with me and offered loads of support throughout the summer. Special thanks to her for reading the manuscript and offering always honest assessments, something not every spouse can or will do. Thanks, Lisa.

Introduction

As any native Minnesotan will proudly tell you, our license plate slogan isn't entirely accurate. It reads LAND OF 10,000 LAKES, an impressive number for sure. But most residents will politely point out that the state has closer to 15,000. This is probably about as close to boasting as any native Minnesotan will ever come. It must be our Scandinavian heritage.

And just as many Minnesotans have a low-key personality, so too do all of our lakes and waterways begin life quietly. Unlike western rivers that begin life dramatically, even violently, as they cascade down steep mountain slopes and through narrow dark canyons, our rivers and lakes enter the world with a barely noticeable gurgle. Minnesota waterways rise from massive marshes or one of our countless prairie or forest lakes and gently flow where the geology dictates. Of course, if you visit the north shore of Lake Superior and watch rivers such as the Temperance and the Cascade tumble wildly through narrow canyons, you'll see behavior that is the opposite of most state streams'.

What Minnesota lacks in vertical scenery it more than makes up in vistas of water. It has countless lakes, ponds, puddles, wetlands, rivers, steams, creeks, and—well, you get the idea. The state has so much water that people in the arid Southwest have cast a covetous eye toward our liquid assets. Consequently, it's no secret that most of the interesting terrain in the state has some relationship with water.

You will notice as you peruse this cycling guide that most of the rides have something to do with water. Most routes circle a lake, follow a river, or roll through a countryside dotted with ponds. When a biker is riding in Minnesota, it's virtually impossible to not ride around or along a body of water.

Whether it's the scenic beauty of the St. Croix Valley, the imposing bluffs of the Mississippi River, the spectacular shoreline of Lake Superior, or a five-acre pond teeming with turtles, egrets, and red-winged blackbirds, water has shaped and continues to shape Minnesota. Though it's possible to find excellent riding almost anywhere in the state, the most scenic rides owe many of their best features to a body of water.

We owe our abundance of lakes to the glaciers that visited Minnesota several times in the past million or so years. They left behind not only piles of debris from Canada, in the form of moraines and eskers, but also thousands of lakes as they melted. And besides ridges of glacial till, meltwater from massive glacial lakes carved the valleys of the three largest rivers in Minnesota: the St. Croix, the Minnesota, and the great river, the Mississippi.

In addition to having an incredible amount of water, Minnesota occupies transition zones that divide east from west and north from south. The state straddles a line that divides the great prairies of the West from the endless hardwood forests of the East. Cutting across this zone, another line separates the fertile farmland of the Corn Belt from the bogs and boreal forests of the North.

As you drive from west to east, rainfall increases and the prairie gradually gives way to ever larger patches of hardwood forest. The landscape slowly changes from one dominated by huge farm fields and small areas of woods to one of smaller fields squeezed among large areas of forest. Eventually, you reach bluff country, an area sculpted by rivers and streams that occupies a narrow band along the eastern border. But even in this rugged area of steep hills and narrow valleys, farmers cultivate almost every tillable acre right to the edge of the Mississippi. Only in the massive forest areas of northeastern and north-central Minnesota does nature finally overcome the plow.

Along the southern edge of this region, agriculture maintains a tenuous relationship with the forest. Smaller and smaller fields occupy the ever shrinking patches of dry land that sits among huge tracts of bog and forest. As you go farther north, you'll notice fields becoming smaller and the mix of crops changing. Finally, the soil becomes too thin and the climate too cool to support anything but scattered fields of forage grass. Besides geology, climate plays an important role in this dramatic change from field to hardwood forest to pine forest.

In addition to occupying two transition zones, Minnesota also sits in a region where weather systems from the North and South collide. Although we don't experience as many violent storms as the southern plains, we have our own weather quirks. Without the benefit of large elevation differences (i.e., mountains), it may be eighty degrees in southern Minnesota and fifty degrees 150 miles north along Lake Superior. Even in areas far removed from the big lake, the weather can change dramatically.

Fortunately for cyclists, however, weather in Minnesota doesn't change as quickly as it can in the mountains. While it may snow a few days after a seventy-degree afternoon, you'll usually experience slower changes.

Throughout this book you will notice many descriptions of green. Dark green, light green, medium green, and just plain green roll along throughout the pages. Green is great, since it makes for scenery that ranges from soothing to vibrant. But this being the North, something has to happen to all the greenery surrounding the roads and trails. "Something" in this case is the cool temperatures of autumn, and gradually the massive monochromatic display becomes a multihued explosion of color.

When the trees and bushes change from their summer wardrobe of green, every ride described takes on a new personality. The lush displays of summer have given way to the colorful showings of plant life bidding good-bye until spring. Besides the visual treats, the odor of decaying leaves fills the air, provoking pleasing memories of jumping in piles of leaves, walking or cycling through forests blanketed with freshly fallen foliage, and feeling excitement at the approach of winter. And with the heat of summer gone, the crisp air of fall awakens the senses.

About the Rides

For this guide I have included many rides in eastern Minnesota, which has some of the best scenery in the state. Almost any ride in this region is scenic because of the St. Croix and Mississippi River Valleys and the numerous tributaries of those rivers. From the apple orchards and endless hills in the southeastern corner to the impenetrable forests of pine and birch that blanket the north shore of Lake Superior, eastern Minnesota has some of the most spectacular scenery in the state.

You will find several routes in Washington County, which is part of the Twin Cities metropolitan area, because of the abundance of quiet country roads, beautiful terrain and proximity to the city. St. Paul and Minneapolis also have a network of bike trails around city lakes and along the Mississippi River. A road ride in rural Washington County presents a dramatic contrast to a cruise around the Minneapolis lakes, and it's hard to believe both are in the metropolitan area.

I have grouped the rides based on their location within four quadrants. For this book I use the same geographic designations Minnesota uses with its bikeways maps. You'll find routes in the northwest, southwest, northeast, and southeast (which includes the Twin Cities) parts of the state. This should help the reader organize rides in specific areas without having to flip all over the book.

Readers may also notice that I haven't included rides from some parts of Minnesota but have included multiple loops in others. Unlike Wisconsin, rural areas of Minnesota don't have nearly so many paved roads. Wisconsin has so many paved roads because of the huge number of dairy farms in the state. Since milk trucks must make daily trips to the farms in all kinds of weather, most roads in dairy country got a coat of blacktop. Minnesota agriculture, however, consists mainly of grain and livestock farms.

With fewer dairy farms, Minnesota never had most of its county roads paved. Although it's always possible to find a great loop in rural Minnesota, if you want to stay on pavement you may have to ride 50 or more miles or do a large part of a loop on a busy highway. While researching routes, I eliminated many possible routes because the only way to keep the mileage within the publisher's established limit was to include an unpaved road with thick, loose gravel. Consequently, I didn't include gravel roads, because they're tough to ride with the narrow tires of a road or touring bike, and not especially fun even with a cross or mountain bike. Moreover, if you've ever been on a gravel road when a car passed throwing up a cloud of dust, you understand why they're lousy for cycling.

Which brings me back to why I didn't include rides in some parts of Minnesota while having multiple rides in others. For example, along the sparsely populated north shore of Lake Superior, it's tough to find many paved county roads. The main one is Highway 61, a busy major highway with good shoulders in a few places and nothing in many other sections. And once you leave the highway, most roads are gravel, making a paved loop almost impossible to find.

This part of Minnesota is perfect for off-road riding, and if you have a mountain bike you'll have many more opportunities to explore the area by bicycle. Because northeastern Minnesota has thousands of acres of national forest, huge wetlands, and few residents, it's no surprise that there aren't many roads crossing the region.

The far northwestern part of Minnesota presents different circumstances. This area has many county roads, but a combination of huge grain farms and sparse population means few paved ones. Moving farther east toward the far north-central area of the state, farms give way to huge tracts of unpopulated wetlands and forest, and even fewer roads. South of this region, however, you'll find thousands of lakes, more people, and more paved roads.

To make up for including few or no rides in a couple of regions, I've mapped multiple routes in others. Besides a cluster of rides in the St. Croix and Mississippi River Valleys, you'll find a group in Stearns County. This central Minnesota county has more dairy farms and consequently has more paved roads than some of the flatter regions with large crop farms. You could spend many days exploring roads in this area.

As you're enjoying the rides in this book, be aware that counties occasionally change road numbers. If you watch your mileage, you should be fine, even if it's off a couple of tenths of a mile from the directions. The maps, while not drawn to scale, should help if any questions on the loop arise during the ride. Experience has taught me that if the directions say I should take a right at this mileage, and even if my cycle computer is off, to take the turn.

Over the past fifteen years, Minnesota has emerged as a leader in converting abandoned railroad beds into multiple-use trails. Most of these nearly flat corridors began with crushed limestone surfaces, while the state gradually worked on paving them. The conversion has progressed to the point where most rail trails in the state have smooth asphalt surfaces from end to end. While an out-and-back trip on a paved trail may seem boring, for families with children it represents a safe alternative to riding with the kids on a county road.

I tried to figure out loops involving rail trails, but often the lack of even a semi-deserted paved road eliminated that option. Although it's not always possible to do a loop when riding these trails, it's surprising how many new features you'll see even on your return trip on an out-and-back excursion. You'll have different views of rivers, bluffs, ponds, and the thick forests that envelop many of these trails, and the return trip may leave you feeling as if you're riding a different trail. Wherever possible, I've included a loop for each rail trail, either as a primary ride, using the trail for a portion, or as an option.

Equipment/Safety

Somewhere during my years of riding and selling bicycles, I heard someone say, "The bike is just the beginning." It may have been a shop employee trying to sell accessories, or an experienced rider helping to outfit a novice. If you ride a lot, you probably have all the gear needed for long rides. If you're new to cycling and plan on touring or doing rides of 20 or more miles, below you'll find a list of accessories that will help make your rides more enjoyable.

Helmets. Though you can delay buying a pump, bag, or repair kit, don't put off getting a helmet. A helmet represents cheap insurance, and when you consider the alternatives it's well worth the $30 or more it will cost. None of us likes to think about crashing, and all of us certainly hope it never happens to us. But it can occur, and spending a few dollars on a helmet now may save you countless thousands later. Of course, it may also save your life. Buy a helmet, and wear it.

Accessories. Besides a helmet, a water-bottle cage and bottle are probably the next most important accessories to buy. Staying hydrated will help you ride longer and stronger, and even if you don't ride long distances, it makes shorter rides more pleasant. For longer distances put two cages on your bike and carry two bottles. Becoming dehydrated can ruin a ride and, in extreme instances, be dangerous. Don't wait to drink until you're thirsty.

You shouldn't need to eat while doing most of the rides in this book. If you want to carry food, the best choices include energy bars, bananas, fig bars, and other items that digest quickly. An energy drink can work well to get you through a short spell of hunger, but try one on a shorter ride before taking it on a longer one.

It's a good idea to have at least a small bike bag to carry a spare tube, a patch kit, keys, a map of the ride, and perhaps a snack and money. Consider a larger bag if you want to carry a light jacket or lunch.

Clothing. If you're reading this you probably plan on riding more than just around the neighborhood. For longer rides, having the right clothing can often mean the difference between a comfortable, pleasant ride and an unpleasant one. A pair of padded bike shorts helps make the seat (of the bike) feel much more comfortable, while a jersey with pockets provides an extra place to carry stuff and helps wick moisture away from your skin. Cycling gloves provide a cushion for hands and protect them in a fall.

If you don't like the tight fit and look of Lycra shorts, you can get baggies that look like casual shorts but have an inner pad where it counts. They're comfortable, and people won't stare at you when you enter that small-town grocery or convenience store.

Eye Protection. Besides protecting your eyes from the sun and making it easier to see, sunglasses may save you from getting a bug or piece of gravel in the eye. I can't count the number of times I've had a bug smack my glasses, and I shudder to think what would have happened without them. Consider buying sport glasses with two lenses, tinted for sunny days and clear for cloudy ones.

Tire Repair. Eventually, you're going to get a flat. It's almost inevitable, especially if you ride a lot. Even if you never do any major work on your bike, at least learn how to change or repair a tube. It's easy to do and can save you from having to walk. Carry a spare tube, a patch kit, a Quick Stik tire lever, a pump, and electrical tape in the unlikely event a tire tears.

Traffic Laws. One of my main peeves continues to be cyclists of all ages, but especially adults, who ignore stop signs and traffic laws as soon as they get on a bike. I believe that these people think of a bike as a toy that isn't subject to the rules of the road. They're wrong. A bike is a vehicle and subject to the rules and laws of the road. Obey traffic laws and use common sense on the road.

Before You Go. Many if not most casual cyclists ride on underinflated tires. Not only do soft tires make pedaling harder; they're more prone to pinch flats. Check your air pressure before every ride, and inspect the tire for glass, metal, or sharp rocks that may cause a flat on the road. Pump tires up to the maximum pressure when riding the road. You'll roll more efficiently and enjoy the ride more.

Ride Name	Best Country	Farm Views	Water Views
1 Apple Blossom Loop	●		
2 Lanesboro to Fountain Loop			●
3 Douglas Trail—Pine Island Loop		●	
4 Red Wing to Frontenac Loop	●		
5 The Poetry Tour	●		
6 Cannon Valley Trail: Red Wing to Welch			●
7 Owatonna—Rice Lake Park Loop		●	
8 The Kenyon Loop		●	
9 Sakatah Lake Loop			●
10 The Afton Loop			
11 Stillwater–Withrow Loop			
12 Marine-on-St. Croix Loop	●		
13 River Road Tour			●
14 Lilydale Park Trail			●
15 Gateway Trail			
16 Farms, Forest, and River Loop	●		
17 Minnehaha Creek to Lake Harriet			●
18 Mille Lacs Lake Loop			●
19 Lakes of Grand Rapids			●
20 Roaming the Range			●
21 Cruising Along Gitchee Gummi			●
22 Touring Tettegouche Country	●		●
23 Route of the Voyageurs	●		●
24 Heartland–Fish Hook Loop			●
25 Detroit Lakes Loop			●
26 Pelican Lake Loop			●
27 Phelps Mill Loop			●
28 Underwood Loop			●
29 Alexandria Loop			●
30 Lake Osakis Loop			●
31 Albany Loop			
32 Avon Loop			
33 Dairy Country Tour			
34 Lake Minnewaska Loop			●
35 Lake Traverse and Prairie Pothole Tour			●
36 Lake That Speaks Loop			●
37 Montevideo Loop		●	
38 Norway and Games Lake Loop			●
39 Prairie View Tour		●	
40 Chanarambie Valley Loop		●	

Best Valleys	Rolling Hills	Family Rides	Wilderness Rides	Romantic	
			●	●	**1**
		● (partial)		●	**2**
		● (partial)			**3**
					4
					5
		●		●	**6**
					7
					8
		●			**9**
●					**10**
	●				**11**
					12
		●			**13**
		●			**14**
	●	●			**15**
				●	**16**
		●			**17**
					18
					19
					20
					21
			●		**22**
			●		**23**
		● (partial)			**24**
					25
					26
					27
					28
					29
		● (partial)			**30**
	●				**31**
	●				**32**
	●				**33**
		● (partial)			**34**
					35
					36
		● (partial)			**37**
					38
					39
					40

Apple Blossom Loop

Distance:	24.2 miles
Approximate Pedaling Time:	2 to 3 hours
Terrain:	Rolling, with one long climb
Traffic:	Light
Surface:	Smooth asphalt, with a 1-mile stretch of gravel that looked as if it was going to be paved soon
Things to See:	Spectacular bluff area along the Mississippi River, apple orchards
Facilities:	Restaurants and convenience store in LaCrescent, small general store in Nodine

In a state dominated by prairie to the west, pine forest to the north, and one of the flattest valleys on earth to the northwest, the terrain on this ride is startling, even stunning in its abruptness. Located in the driftless region of Minnesota, a land that the last glacier missed, limestone bluffs soar hundreds of feet above the Mississippi River. The ravine-lined cliffs that border the river divide the flat river bottomlands from the relentlessly rolling landscape above.

In a region that featured land too rugged for row crops and a climate that for a northern state is temperate, apples became one of the main crops. If you ride this loop in the spring, you'll see where it got its name. While apple trees cling to the steep sides of the valley, lush fields of corn and alfalfa occupy the less severe pitches that slope gradually away from the river.

This loop begins in LaCrescent, a town known for—what else?—apples. From the town park follow CR 6 as it winds

Ride 1: Apple Blossom Loop

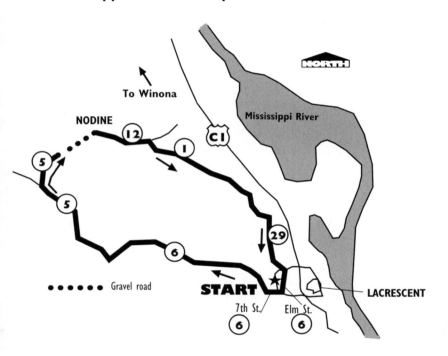

Getting There

From the Twin Cities take Highway 61 to LaCrescent. Exit at the stoplight at the main intersection in town, proceed for several blocks, and turn left onto Elm Street. Go to South 7th and turn right to town park and pool.

DIREC-TIONS at a glance

0.0	Start at LaCrescent park and pool—turn right onto South 7th (CR 6).
7.9	Changes to CR 5 at Winona County line.
10.5	Right to stay on CR 5.
15.4	Right onto CR 1.
22.3	Changes to CR 29 at Houston County line.
23.8	Go straight as road becomes CR 6 and Elm Street.
24.1	Right onto South 7th (CR 6).
24.2	Return to park.

through narrow valleys on its journey away from the Mississippi. While making the long climb along this road, you'll begin to understand why this area is susceptible to flash floods. Yet unlike other steep-sided ravines, this valley has enough flat area to support lush fields of row crops. As you pedal through the intense green landscape, you may notice the steady uphill pitch that resembles the grade of a rail trail.

At 7.9 miles the road changes to CR 5; at 10.5 miles turn right to stay on it. At 11.5 miles the surface changes to gravel at the base of a steep hill but changes back to blacktop 1 mile later. In August 1997 it looked as if the county was getting ready to pave this short stretch. If you don't like to climb, you can smile at the top of this hill—it's the last major ascent of the ride.

At 13.6 miles you'll come to Nodine, a small town that may leave you wondering how such tiny places survive. After a stretch of rough pavement that CR 5 and CR 12 share, turn right on CR 1 for a well-deserved cycling treat. This road features smooth pavement and excellent shoulders. As if that weren't enough for a cyclist, this country lane also has some of the best views in Minnesota. It may be difficult, but try to keep your eyes on the road as the panorama of the river valley far below unfolds. As I rode along the sweet pavement that hugged the edge of the massive bluff, I suddenly knew how an eagle must feel soaring above the great river.

Within a couple of miles of turning onto CR 1, you'll come upon the appropriately named Sudden Valley. At 21.2 miles be sure to stop at the scenic overlook and take in the amazing view of the Mississippi and the rolling terrain of Wisconsin spread out far below and in front of you. I'm going to take the easy way out and just say that more words won't do justice to this vista.

At 21.6 miles you'll start a steep descent through exposed rock cliffs to LaCrescent. Remember the long climb out of town? Here's your reward. Enjoy it, but don't get too crazy; on a road bike you could reach 60 mph after the initial curves. Locals may wonder about the strange grin on your face as you cruise back to the park. You could try to explain, but they probably wouldn't understand.

Lanesboro to Fountain Loop

Distance:	20.7 miles
Approximate Pedaling Time:	2 to 3 hours
Terrain:	Flat on bike trail, hilly on county roads
Traffic:	Light
Surface:	Smooth asphalt
Things to See:	Root River Valley, scenic farmland, scenic town of Lanesboro
Facilities:	Restrooms, water, restaurants, coffee shop, bike rental, and shopping at or near Lanesboro trailhead; restrooms at Fountain

In a state composed of thousands of square miles of flat farmland and thousands more of isolated pine forest, the hilly terrain of southeastern Minnesota presents a sharp contrast. This part of the state lies in a region known as the driftless area, an island of rocky uplands that covers 10,000 square miles in Minnesota, Wisconsin, Iowa, and Illinois. The area sits on a massive limestone plateau that the last glaciers missed while shaping the surrounding landscape. As the glaciers receded, torrents of meltwater poured into streams and rivers, carving deep valleys.

As the first area settled in Minnesota, parts of the region sustained severe damage from indiscriminate logging and poor farming practices. Today southeastern Minnesota remains an area of craggy bluffs, steep-sided ravines, clear trout streams, and patches of farmland. Since much of this land now lies in the Richard J. Dorer Memorial Hardwood Forest, hills once scarred

by erosion have regained much of their former grandeur. Covered by a carpet of intense green in spring and summer, the hills show off with an explosion of colors during autumn.

Lanesboro, the origin of this ride, sits snugly between bluffs along the Root River, in one of the only areas populated by Amish in Minnesota. The Root River Trail follows a railroad bed as it links several small towns in this scenic area. For riders who don't like to climb, this mostly flat trail provides the perfect way to tour the deep valleys and steep hills of the region. And Lanesboro, with its many historic inns and guest houses, makes an excellent base from which to explore this rugged country.

This ride begins at the Lanesboro trailhead, which sits in the center of the compact and comfortable downtown. Unlike other trails, this one has an information center with real restrooms, a restaurant, and a bike shop next door. Lanesboro is the type of town that invites you with its layout to walk the sidewalks or cycle along the main street for postride refreshments or browsing.

From the trailhead simply follow the trail west as it gradually climbs out of the valley to Fountain. *Climbing* is a relative term. While professional bike racers would tell stories of epic European ascents that stretch for miles at lung-bursting grades, casual cyclists might talk about that block-long bump at the end of their street. Fortunately, rail-trail grades fall well within the realm of casual riders. This trail has one of the more noticeable grades, especially for the last half-mile before Fountain, where it climbs out of the valley.

At 4.8 miles you'll come to an intersection with the Preston–Harmony Trail, which runs 5.5 miles to Preston. The main trail continues winding along the river, passing under canopies of trees, through open meadows, and past neat farms. Besides the sights, you'll experience the smells of manure and silage and the sounds of cattle. At 11 miles you'll reach the Fountain trailhead and turn right onto CR 8, which runs along the northern ridge of the valley. As in most of southeastern Minnesota, from the top of these ridges you'll experience incredible views of the surrounding countryside.

Ride 2: Lanesboro to Fountain Loop

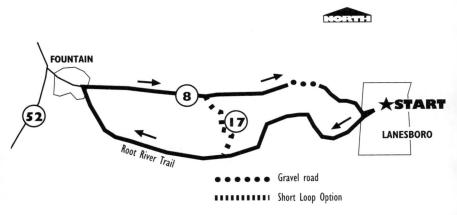

●●●●●● Gravel road

▮▮▮▮▮▮▮▮▮▮ Short Loop Option

Getting There

From the Twin Cities go south on Highway 52 to Fountain and take CR 8 east to Lanesboro. Park in Sylvan Park (1 block from trailhead) or in lot along trail.

DIRECTIONS at a glance

0.0 Follow the Root River Trail west.
4.8 Intersection with Preston–Harmony Trail.
5.2 Cross CR 17.
11.0 From Fountain trailhead turn right onto CR 8.
20.7 Return to Lanesboro.

Short loop option:
5.2 Turn right onto CR 17. (You'll face an immediate 1.2-mile climb.)
6.9 Turn right onto CR 8.
12.7 Return to Lanesboro.

After a rolling ride that mostly ascends, you'll come to a short descent that feeds into a sweeping right curve, followed by a left and one final short climb. You're about to receive your reward for climbing: a screaming descent through the bluffs back to Lanesboro. Enjoy it, but as the road curves left at the bottom watch for traffic entering from a road on your right. To finish cross Parkway Street to the trailhead and wipe the tears from your eyes.

3 Douglas Trail– Pine Island Loop

Distance:	17.2 miles
Approximate Pedaling Time:	1 to 2 hours
Terrain:	Flat rail trail and county road with rolling hills
Traffic:	Light
Surface:	Asphalt (cracked on trail, mostly smooth on roads)
Things to See:	Rolling farmland, creek valleys with pockets of hardwood forest
Facilities:	Restrooms at park in Pine Island, convenience stores and restaurants in downtown (1 block from park), parking and soda machine in Douglas at 8.1 miles

Occasionally, a cyclist stumbles on a perfect ride. It doesn't happen often, but when it does the temptation exists to do it over and over. For this ride there is good news and there is bad news. The bad news is that it isn't the perfect loop—it's close, but it doesn't make it. The good news is that it has something for every rider.

In a landscape of never-ending hills, the Douglas Trail provides a flat, traffic-free alternative for nonclimbers or small children. Although this trail doesn't sit in a river valley as other state trails do, it still provides a relaxing way to enjoy a cruise through farm country. For riders who like to climb, or at least can tolerate ascending, the county road that crosses the trail twice offers the option of two separate loops instead of a single

Ride 3: Douglas Trail–Pine Island Loop

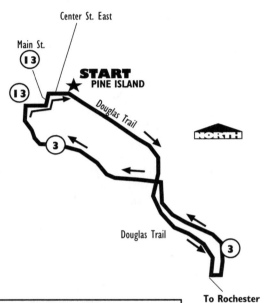

Center St. East

Main St.

13

13

START
PINE ISLAND

Douglas Trail

3

NORTH

Douglas Trail

3

To Rochester

Getting There

From the Twin Cities take Highway
52 south to Pine Island. From Main
Street, turn left onto Center Street
East and go about 1 block to the park.

DIREC-TIONS
at a glance

0.0 Start at Pine Island town park.
5.1 CR 3 intersection (see below).
8.1 Turn left onto CR 3.
8.3 Turn left to stay on CR 3.
11.6 Turn left to stay on CR 3.
11.8 Douglas Trail.
16.5 Turn right onto CR 13 (8th Street Southwest).
17.1 Turn right onto Center Street East.
17.2 Arrive at park.

Short loop option:
5.1 Turn right at CR 3.
9.8 Turn right onto CR 13 (8th Street Southwest).
10.4 Turn right onto Center Street East.
10.5 Arrive at park.

---

out-and-back. For those who measure success by notching destinations, the trail ends on the outskirts of Rochester, home of the Mayo Clinic and one of the largest cities in Minnesota.

The northern trailhead begins in Pine Island, a clean little town whose compact downtown is a short walk from the trail. With grass growing in cracks, it doesn't take a rider long to figure out that this path doesn't see as much use as other state trails. Instead of winding with the river, this trail runs straight as a ruler, with only a few, almost imperceptible curves.

The views from the trail are pleasant, with clumps of hardwood forest poking up like heads of broccoli above lush fields of corn and soybeans. At 5.1 miles the trail crosses CR 3 and presents the first option for a loop. If you don't care to climb and want to do a loop, turn right and follow the road back to Pine Island. Riders who desire a longer loop, don't mind a couple of climbs, and want to get out of the valley for some incredible views should stay on the trail.

At 8.1 miles the trail crosses CR 3 again, this time in Douglas, a rather motley collection of old houses and defunct businesses. Turn left onto CR 3, and left again at 8.3 miles to stay on it. The first sight that presents itself is a hill that looks like two giant steps. It may appear daunting at first but it's a gentle grade, and the short, level section in the middle lets the legs recover. The smooth pavement and graceful curves of this road are a welcome change from the sometimes rough and continually straight trail.

Upon cresting this first hill, the road winds and dips past some farms before another short climb leads to about a half-mile-long descent. The problem at the top of this hill is choosing between stopping and taking in the beautiful view or keeping that precious momentum for a faster trip down the long hill. Whatever decision you make will delight one of the senses: Stop and you'll treat the eyes to a panorama of rolling hills; opt for speed and your ears will express gratitude at the wind whistling through them.

After the descent turn left at 11.6 miles to stay on CR 3, which crosses the trail 0.2 mile later. The next 5 miles feature a barely noticeable ascent, followed by two short climbs that may test your legs if you've been riding hard. When you reach the top of this notch in the ridge, your reward awaits: a gradual descent, followed by a flat finish. At 16.5 miles turn right onto CR 13 and enjoy a cool-down spin through town.

Red Wing to Frontenac Loop

Distance:	24.5 miles
Approximate Pedaling Time:	2 to 3 hours
Terrain:	Rolling, with one long climb
Traffic:	Moderate to heavy on Highway 61 (has wide shoulder), moderate on Highway 58, light elsewhere
Surface:	Smooth asphalt
Things to See:	Bluff area along the Mississippi River, rolling farmland, Frontenac, Lake Pepin
Facilities:	Restaurants, convenience stores, and shopping in Red Wing

Historical and recent events along the Mississippi River constantly remind us of the power of water. The river flows through a valley carved deep by incredible amounts of water from the Glacial River Warren aeons ago. After starting from Glacial Lake Aggasiz, which was larger than all the Great Lakes combined, the huge river first carved out the Minnesota River Valley before merging with waters from the upper Mississippi and St. Croix Rivers. To complete the process, the Mississippi partly filled the broad valley with several hundred feet of silt after the massive flood. As a current reminder of who is boss, the river still overruns its banks, despite the efforts of human beings. It's a humbling display of power.

Frontenac State Park, which occupies the site of the abandoned river town of Frontenac, has a long, rich history. Archaeological research estimates that the first human beings lived in the area from 400 B.C. to A.D. 300. The first Europeans reached

the area in 1680, with the first settlement built in 1727. As steamboat traffic steadily increased through the 1800s, Frontenac became one of the most popular summer vacation resorts in the country. Human influence aside, the park remains an excellent place to watch bird migration, with bald and golden eagles common visitors during winter. Timber rattlesnakes also live in the bluffs of the park, which is one of the only places in Minnesota with habitat suitable for them.

The ride begins at Twin Bluff Middle School in Red Wing and, appropriately for a ride in river-valley country, has a climb within a half-mile. This is an excellent way to get through Red Wing, since it bypasses the busy downtown area. At 1.4 miles turn left onto Highway 58 and enjoy the smooth pavement and 1-mile descent. Try not to get too carried away with this downhill, because near the bottom you turn right onto Bush Street, at 3.0 miles.

This section of smooth, quiet pavement isn't an official through street for motor vehicles, but for bikes it's a good way to avoid a busy part of town. At 4.7 miles turn right onto Highway 61, the busiest segment of the loop. On weekends, especially during autumn, it carries a steady stream of traffic. The road has a wide shoulder, and you'll have many scenic river bluffs to enjoy.

At 12.4 miles you'll enter the tiny settlement of Frontenac and turn right onto CR 2, which will take you into a different world. You will trade a busy highway for a quiet county road and will leave a broad valley floor framed by imposing rock bluffs to enter a narrower one with walls softened by thick forests of hardwood. Rows of crops and neat farms complete the change from hectic highway to idyllic countryside. And, of course, as you leave the basin of the Mississippi you'll start climbing on the mostly gentle grade of CR 2. But this changes on the next section.

After turning right onto CR 5 at 17.1 miles and following a gradual warm-up ascent, the road tilts up for 1.3 miles. As the road climbs this final ridge, you'll leave the intimate feeling of

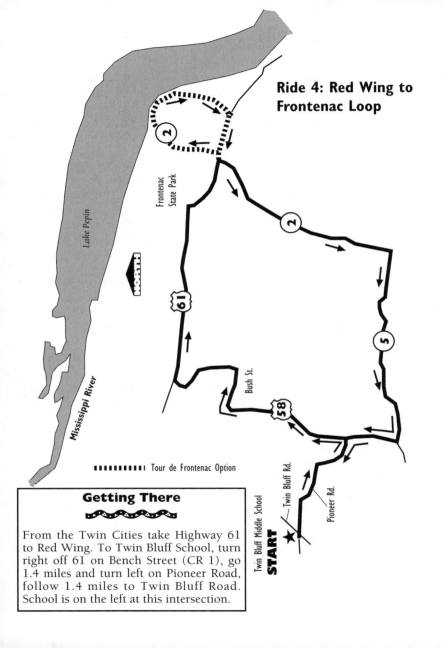

Ride 4: Red Wing to Frontenac Loop

Lake Pepin

Frontenac State Park

Mississippi River

NORTH

61

2

2

5

58

Bush St.

Twin Bluff Rd.

Pioneer Rd.

Twin Bluff Middle School

START

IIIIIIIIII Tour de Frontenac Option

Getting There

From the Twin Cities take Highway 61 to Red Wing. To Twin Bluff School, turn right off 61 on Bench Street (CR 1), go 1.4 miles and turn left on Pioneer Road, follow 1.4 miles to Twin Bluff Road. School is on the left at this intersection.

DIREC-TIONS at a glance

0.0 Start at Twin Bluff Middle School and turn left onto Pioneer Road.
1.4 Left onto Highway 58.
3.0 Right onto Bush Street.
4.1 Veer left through golf course parking lot.
4.7 Right onto Highway 61.
12.4 Right onto CR 2.
17.1 Right onto CR 5.
21.7 Right onto Highway 58.
23.1 Left onto Pioneer Road.
24.5 Return to school.

Tour de Frontenac option:
12.5 Left onto CR 2.
15.8 Right onto Frontage Road.
15.9 Right onto Highway 61.
17.5 Left onto CR 2.
22.2 Right onto CR 5.
26.8 Right onto Highway 58.
28.2 Left onto Pioneer Road.
29.6 Return to school.

the valley for the open and rolling highlands of Goodhue County. Few other places in Minnesota offer such a dramatic contrast. As you reach the crest, a panoramic view unfolds of wooded ravines, convex fields of corn, and farms sitting on distant ridges or snuggled into quiet glens.

At 21.7 miles turn right onto Highway 58 for the short jaunt back to Red Wing. At 23.1 miles turn left onto Pioneer Road and one final hill—a welcome descent this time—before finishing.

Tour de Frontenac option

This option will take you into the residential area of Frontenac and past the entrance to the state park. It's fun to explore the town, with its houses that look as if they haven't changed in a hundred years. Many streets still remain unpaved, and this route treats riders to a spectacular view of Lake Pepin and the Wisconsin shore.

The Poetry Tour

Distance:	21.4 miles
Approximate Pedaling Time:	2 to 3 hours
Terrain:	Rolling, with one long climb
Traffic:	Moderate on CR 1, Highway 19, and Highway 61; light elsewhere
Surface:	Mostly smooth asphalt
Things to See:	Four poetry barns, scenic rolling farmland and valleys
Facilities:	Restaurants, convenience stores, and shopping in Red Wing

To hardy and conservative Midwest farmers, barns usually represent function over form. For generations farmers have used barns to store bales of hay and shelter livestock. They'd slap a coat of red paint on a barn every five or so years and maybe repair the occasional rotten board. Though most barns were built with simple lines, some builders added decorative features that changed them from structures of functional elegance to works of rural art.

In 1983 a poet from Massachusetts persuaded four Red Wing farmers to let him paint a poem about one of the four seasons on each of their barns. After choosing ten possibilities, the poet surprisingly found that the first four farmers he approached said he could paint the verses on their barns. Of the four works three remain intact, with the winter poem partly covered by an addition to that barn. Although the verses have all faded after thirteen years, each remains legible on its unique canvas.

The ride begins at Twin Bluff Middle School, with a spin along the smooth pavement of Pioneer Road. After a fun but short downhill, you'll reach CR 1 at 1.4 miles. Turn left onto CR

1 and ready yourself for a long climb out of the river valley. Although this ascent measures about 2 miles, it's gradual until the last half-mile or so, where the road rears up at a steeper angle. CR 1 has moderately heavy truck traffic on weekdays, so you may want to ride it on a weekend or in the early evening.

Just after cresting Featherstone Hill, you'll see the barn with the first poem, which depicts autumn. All the barns stand out, but this one is especially prominent, due to its size and its location on the top of a hill. After a couple of small rolling hills, turn right on CR 6 at 7.7 miles and prepare to enjoy the best section of the ride. Most of the remaining grades descend, and smooth pavement, along with light traffic, awaits you on the next 4.5 miles.

Just after turning onto CR 6, you'll see the second poetry barn on your right, this one with a verse about spring. Immediately after this barn you'll face a couple of moderate rollers, before reaching an exhilarating descent, at about 9.6 miles. As the sinuous road continues back to the valley floor, you'll pass fields of corn and soybeans that follow the contours of hillsides in graceful curves, before cutting through limestone bluffs near the bottom. From the top of this highlands area, you'll have panoramic views of the ravines that long ago carved this region.

At 12.2 miles turn right onto Highway 19, and soon thereafter look on your left to see what remains of the winter poem on the third barn. Though Highway 19 has moderate traffic, the smooth pavement and a narrow shoulder make it a decent route as you continue descending toward the Mississippi. Near Lierbach Road you'll see the summer verse on the fourth barn, which sits tucked snugly at the base of a long ridge. At 14.9 miles turn right onto Highway 61, which has a wide shoulder, or follow the paved bike path that parallels the highway. The mileage from riding the bike path may vary slightly, but choosing the path will keep you away from the noise and traffic of the highway.

At 18.6 miles turn right onto CR 1 for a short trip past several businesses, including a tannery. Turn left on Pioneer Road at 20.0 miles, endure one short climb, and you're back at the school.

Ride 5: The Poetry Tour

Mississippi River

NORTH

61

19

START

RED WING

Twin Bluff Rd.

Pioneer Rd.

6

1

Getting There

From the Twin Cities take Highway 61 to Red Wing. To reach Twin Bluff Middle School, turn right off Highway 61 onto Bench Street (CR 1), go 1.4 miles, and turn left onto Pioneer Road, follow Pioneer Road 1.4 miles to Twin Bluff Road. School is on the left at this intersection.

DIREC-TIONS at a glance

0.0 Start at Twin Bluff Middle School and turn right onto Pioneer Road.

1.4 Turn left onto CR 1.

7.7 Turn right onto CR 6.

12.2 Turn right onto Highway 19.

14.9 Turn right onto Highway 61 or the bike path.

18.6 Turn right onto CR 1.

20.0 Turn left onto Pioneer Road.

21.4 Return to school.

Cannon Valley Trail:
Red Wing to Welch

Distance:	19.6 miles
Approximate Pedaling Time:	1.5 to 3 hours
Terrain:	Nearly flat rail trail ($2.00 daily fee for adults, children free)
Traffic:	None on trail; light to moderate on CR 1; light elsewhere
Surface:	Smooth asphalt
Things to See:	Picturesque Cannon River Valley, scenic farmland, Mississippi River town of Red Wing, Lake Pepin
Facilities:	Outhouse, convenience store, restaurants, and shopping at and near trailhead in Red Wing; deli, ice cream, and coffee at Welch General Store in Welch

Flowing east through the fertile farmland of southeastern Minnesota, the Cannon River joins the Mississippi near the historic town of Red Wing. Before merging with the big river, the Cannon cuts a scenic path through the bluffs and ravines of this rugged area of the state. Tinted a medium brown, the Cannon looks like a river of chocolate milk, and creative types might imagine the dark green of the surrounding hills as scoops of mint ice cream.

Red Wing sits at the northern end of Lake Pepin, a huge bulge in the Mississippi that offers cyclists looking for serious mileage a 70-mile loop along the Wisconsin and Minnesota sides of the river. Even if you choose not to ride around the lake, it's worth driving around while you are in the area.

Starting on the north side of Red Wing, the Cannon Valley

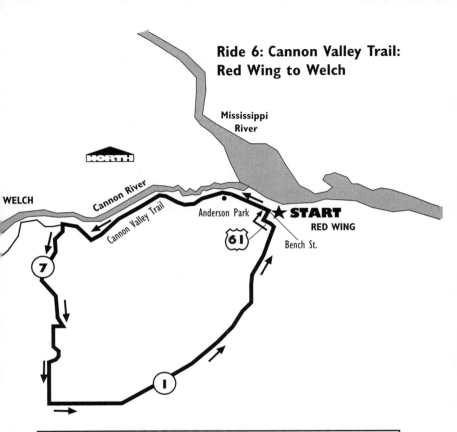

Ride 6: Cannon Valley Trail: Red Wing to Welch

Mississippi River

NORTH

Cannon River

WELCH

Cannon Valley Trail

Anderson Park

61

Bench St.

★ **START**

RED WING

7

1

Getting There

From the Twin Cities take Highway 61 to Red Wing. The trailhead is located at Bench and Main Streets on the north end of Red Wing. Take the first right past the stoplights at CR 1 (Bench Street). There is a sign for the Cannon Valley Trail, and the road crosses under Highway 61 and intersects with Main Street. Turn left onto Main Street and follow it to the trailhead.

An alternative starting point is at Anderson Park, located farther north. Look for signs for the trail after passing the intersection of Highways 61 and 19. A spur trail leads from this park to the Cannon Valley Trail.

DIREC-TIONS at a glance

0.0	Start at Bench and Main Streets trailhead.
3.5	Cannon Valley Archeological Site.
9.8	Welch trailhead and town of Welch.
19.1	Cannon Falls trailhead.

Climber's Loop

0.0	Start at Bench and Main Streets trailhead.
8.8	Turn left onto CR 7.
14.2	Turn right to stay on CR 7.
14.5	Cross Highway 19.
17.7	Turn left onto CR 1.
29.9	Turn left onto Highway 61.
30.1	Turn right onto Bench Street and return to trailhead.

Trail runs west about 20 miles, to the town of Cannon Falls. The trail winds through tunnels of green on a nearly flat converted railroad bed, making it a perfect jaunt for casual cyclists and families. I rode it on a weekday and passed several families with children. Rail trails work well for families because the absence of motor vehicles eliminates one worry for parents, and route finding is extremely easy. Moreover, it's easy to turn back at any time if a rider gets tired, as opposed to having to finish a loop.

If you have the time, Red Wing is a great place to spend a weekend. The historic St. James Hotel, located downtown, makes a unique and convenient base for a day or two of cycling around the area. Because of the numerous old spacious homes in town, it's easy to find a bed-and-breakfast if you prefer lodging that has a more personal touch.

From the parking area at Bench and Main Streets, the path

runs northwest for a couple of miles and provides riders with occasional glimpses of the bluffs of Wisconsin that line the Mississippi. The wide valley contains thousands of acres of wetlands formed by the confluence of the two rivers and offers a strong contrast to the imposing hills that border the river.

The trail gradually swings west to follow the Cannon River. The valley narrows dramatically, and at times you'll feel as if you've entered a tunnel, albeit one painted various shades of green with occasional skylights. Riders will find many benches at scenic areas along the trail. I attempted to count them but lost track somewhere around ten. Besides not being good at math, I was so relaxed and oblivious to anything that wasn't black asphalt or green foliage that I missed some that sat in little clearings overlooking the river. The smooth pavement, quiet surroundings, and lack of weekend crowds will do that to a cyclist on a rail trail.

Without the whoosh of passing cars and trucks, it's easy to get lost in a strange mix of relaxation and endorphin release, brought on by a smooth cadence and soothing scenery. The gentle grades of rail trails are deceiving at times. You'll look at the trail and think it's flat, while your legs and gear ratios tell you it's not.

At 9.8 miles the trail reaches its halfway point, at Welch. Known for the local ski area and as a base for canoeing on the river, this tiny village makes a perfect rest stop. A visit to the Welch General Store will refuel riders for the gentle descent back to Red Wing. Cyclists looking for a longer ride can take the trail to Cannon Falls, an option that will increase total mileage to nearly 40 miles.

Climber's Loop

I call this option the Climber's Loop because when you turn onto CR 7 at Welch, you'll face almost 5 miles of continual climbing. Most of the grades aren't steep, but there's no doubt that you're pedaling uphill. I would not ride CR 1 on weekdays or during harvesttime, because of heavy grain-truck traffic at these times. A local friend rides it on weekends and weeknights and says it's much quieter then.

7 Owatonna–Rice Lake Park Loop

Distance:	22 miles
Approximate Pedaling Time:	1.5 to 2 hours
Terrain:	Mostly flat, with a couple of short hills
Traffic:	Mostly light; moderate close to town
Surface:	Smooth asphalt
Things to See:	Rice Lake State Park, scenic prairie
Facilities:	Food, lodging, and groceries in Owatonna; restrooms and water at Manthey Park

Owatonna sits amid some of the most fertile farmland in Minnesota, close to an area that marked the transition zone between prairie to the west and deciduous forest to the east. The town got its name from Owatonna, the frail daughter of Chief Wabena who, legend says, regained her health by drinking from a local healing spring, or *minnewaucan*. Today the town is home to the headquarters of several large companies and is a hub of commerce for the surrounding area.

Rice Lake State Park, located east of town, has several interesting features that make it worth visiting. As happened in much of Minnesota, glaciers were instrumental in forming this lake and the surrounding landscape. The park sits in the aforementioned transition zone, which formed a large area called the southern oak barrens. This is the rarest type of native vegetation left in Minnesota.

Because of its shallow depth and marshy edges, Rice Lake played a key role in the lives of Indians and still does in the

migration of waterfowl. From the lake Indians harvested wild rice, which gave the lake its name, though wild rice no longer grows in it. A headwater source of the Zumbro River, Rice Lake is the only good-size lake for many miles, and it's an important stop for migrating birds. Besides waterfowl, the varied habitat attracts many other birds, including up to seven species of woodpecker. Visiting prairie parks may give you a new perspective on the beauty and significance of grasslands, especially if you've found yourself bored while traveling through endless farm fields.

Starting on the north side of town, this ride for the first 2 miles goes through a suburban area that looks like any other suburban area. CR 34 is wide, but it's close to a gravel pit and carries a steady stream of truck traffic on weekdays. At 1.8 miles turn right onto CR 8, and at 2.3 miles turn left onto CR 35, which takes you out of town. The road is narrow and may be busy for the first 2 miles but gets quieter after passing the golf course.

After crossing CR 43, the road winds through the usual fields of row crops, but you may notice on the right a section of rolling prairie broken only by clumps of hardwoods and an occasional house. It's startling to see such a large chunk of uncultivated land sitting among acre after acre of corn and soybeans. Not part of the park, this land is a combination of old pasture and creek bottom too wet to farm.

After a short section on CR 37, you'll turn right onto CR 19 and ride along a shallow ridge on the north edge of the state park. Though you can't see the lake from the road, you will see remnants of the oak barrens that once covered the area. This road in the mid-1800s was a stagecoach route that ran through the town of Rice Lake. The little village never prospered, and the rise of the railroads sealed the fate of the stagecoach trail.

At the entrance to the park, the road tilts gently down as it winds west back toward Owatonna. Before reaching the second golf course you pass on this loop, you'll drop into a creek valley and face the longest climb of the loop. The next hill you en-

Ride 7: Owatonna–Rice Lake Park Loop

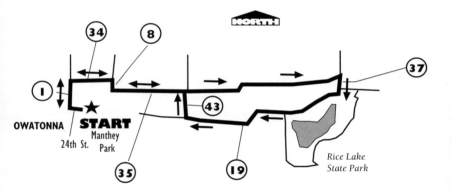

Getting There

From St. Paul or Minneapolis take I–35 south to Owatonna. Exit on CR 34 and turn left; follow CR 34 to CR 1 (North Cedar) and turn right; go about 0.2 mile and turn left on 24th Street, which is the entrance to Manthey Park.

DIREC-TIONS at a glance

0.0 Depart Manthey Park.
0.1 Turn right onto CR 1 (Cedar Avenue).
0.3 Turn right onto CR 34.
1.8 Turn right onto CR 8.
2.3 Turn left onto CR 35.
10.1 Turn right onto CR 37.
10.7 Turn right onto CR 19.
16.1 Turn right onto CR 43.
17.2 Turn left onto CR 35.
19.7 Turn right onto CR 8.
20.2 Turn left onto CR 34.
21.7 Turn left onto CR 1.
21.9 Turn left onto 24th Street.
22.0 Return to park.

Short loop option:

0.0 From Rice Lake State Park, turn left on CR 19.
4.4 Turn right onto CR 43.
5.5 Turn right onto CR 35.
10.8 Turn right onto CR 37.
11.4 Turn right onto CR 19.
12.4 Turn left back to the state park.

counter is on CR 43, and this one descends quickly, providing a perfect launch for the short uphill that follows. After playing on the hills, you'll reach CR 35, where you turn left for the trip back to town.

The Kenyon Loop

Distance:	20.6 miles
Approximate Pedaling Time:	1.5 to 3 hours
Terrain:	Rolling, with a couple of gradual climbs
Traffic:	Light
Surface:	Smooth asphalt
Things to See:	Neat rural town, scenic farmland
Facilities:	Restroom, vending machines, picnic area, swimming pool in town park; restaurants and convenience stores in town

Located only an hour south of the Twin Cities, this area of fertile farmland represents a transition zone of sorts. Situated about halfway between the broad valleys of the Mississippi and Minnesota Rivers, the area features a blend of short rolling hills and farm fields carved out of nearly flat prairie. Numerous creeks have cut their way through the landscape on their journey to the big rivers, leaving narrow wooded valleys north of town, while to the south fields stretch out for miles, broken only by patches of trees guarding farm buildings.

Although Kenyon and surrounding towns have in recent years attracted urban refugees who commute to their jobs in the cities, there's no doubt that you're in farm country.

Prosperous farms dot the crests of hills, as row crops wrap in sinuous lines around the gentle hillsides. A farmer will raise his hand in a modest Minnesota greeting as he pulls a plow through the thick carpet of green, turning it into a dark brownish black. And the aroma of freshly turned topsoil—rich, dark, and full of humus—mingles with the sweet smell of clover and freshly cut alfalfa, forming a pleasant rural perfume.

This loop begins in the Kenyon town park, a perfect base from which to explore the countryside. The park has a pool, mature shade trees, and a picnic area, making it an ideal place to leave noncycling friends or family while the riders hit the road. After rolling through the neat downtown, CR 12 curves gently before climbing a short hill. The crest provides a beautiful view of Goodhue County as it rolls toward the Mississippi. If you've ever flown over the Midwest and marveled at the seemingly infinite amount of farmland rolling by far below, the view from here offers a more intimate picture of this vast display of agriculture.

CR 12 runs almost straight east, rolling over a few more gradual hills before meeting CR 1 at 6.0 miles. Don't worry about that hill ahead: You'll turn right well before it on CR 1, which is mostly flat. Even though this route goes through a landscape of rolling hills, none are the short and steep ones common in river valleys. Instead, they're long, gentle, and only slightly steeper than rail-trail grades.

At 9.8 miles turn right onto CR 11. Looking southeast at this intersection, you'll have an interesting view of huge fields dropping away from the slight high spot you're on. After crossing Highway 56 at 13.5 miles, continue riding west on CR 11. You'll turn right on CR 13 at 15.9 miles and notice immediately that the road tilts up. It's not severe, but there's no doubt the road ascends. This climb and the next one are the types that you would barely feel with a tailwind but seem endless with a headwind. There's a short break between hills, and after you reach the top of the second one it's gradually downhill and flat back to town.

At 19.7 miles turn left onto Highway 56, which at this point has a shoulder and a 30-mph speed limit. Turn left onto 2nd Street at 20.1 miles, and follow it through town to Washington Avenue, where you'll turn right, at 20.5 miles. Another 0.1 mile brings you back to the town park and a refreshing dip in the pool. I'd call that the perfect end to a perfect ride.

Ride 8: The Kenyon Loop

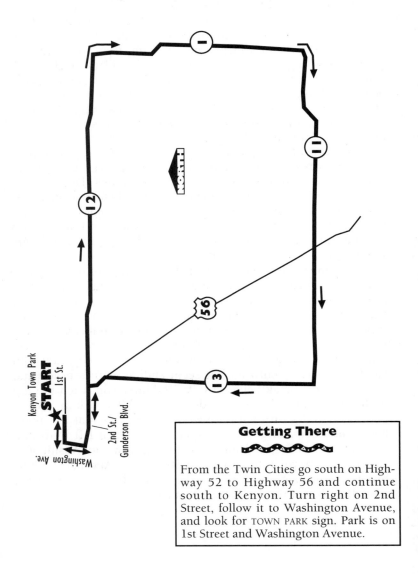

Getting There

From the Twin Cities go south on Highway 52 to Highway 56 and continue south to Kenyon. Turn right on 2nd Street, follow it to Washington Avenue, and look for TOWN PARK sign. Park is on 1st Street and Washington Avenue.

**DIREC-
TIONS
at a glance**

0.0 Turn right onto 1st Street from Kenyon town park.

0.0 Turn left onto Washington Avenue.

0.1 Turn left onto Gunderson Boulevard (2nd Street).

0.4 Go straight at this intersection onto CR 12.

6.0 Right onto CR 1.

9.8 Right onto CR 11.

13.5 Cross Highway 56.

15.9 Right onto CR 13.

19.7 Left onto Highway 56.

20.1 Left onto 2nd Street.

20.5 Right onto Washington Avenue.

20.6 Right onto 1st Street and arrive at park.

Sakatah Lake Loop

Distance:	11.6 miles
Approximate Pedaling Time:	1 hour
Terrain:	Flat
Traffic:	None on trail; light on roads
Surface:	Smooth asphalt
Things to See:	Sakatah Lake State Park
Facilities:	Water and outhouse in Waterville at parking area, convenience store close, water and restrooms in state park

The scenery of this area of rolling prairie comes to us again courtesy of glaciers. Glacial activity shaped this region some 14,000 years ago by leaving behind piles of rock debris called moraines. As the glacier retreated, huge blocks of ice broke off and formed depressions; these became the lakes that now dot the landscape. As you look at the lakes, try to imagine the size of the ice chunks that dimpled the surface enough to make a permanent body of water.

Lake Sakatah is a wide spot in the Cannon River, which is one of the major rivers in southeastern Minnesota. If you've cycled the Cannon Valley Trail, you've seen where this river cuts through the steep forested hills of the Big Woods area near the Mississippi. Here the Cannon meanders aimlessly through small rolling hills as it drops slowly but ever steadily toward the great river.

Members of the Dakota Nation, the Wahpekita tribe, originally lived in this area and used it for hunting, trapping, and gathering. The name *Sakatah* translates to "Singing Hills," and it's fun to let your imagination run again, only this time as it

Ride 9: Sakatah Lake Loop

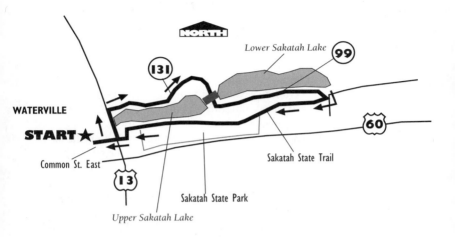

NORTH

Lower Sakatah Lake

99

131

WATERVILLE

START ★

Common St. East

13

Sakatah State Trail

Sakatah State Park

Upper Sakatah Lake

60

Getting There

From St. Paul or Minneapolis, take I–35 south to Faribault. Go west on Highway 60 about 14 miles to Waterville. Turn right onto Highway 13, go about a quarter-mile and turn left onto Common Street East. Park by the basketball court or tennis courts on the other side of the building.

0.0 Take Common Street East from parking area to Highway 13.

0.1 Turn left onto Highway 13.

0.7 Turn right onto CR 131.

3.1 Road changes to CR 99 at county line.

6.6 Turn right onto Sakatah State Trail.

11.5 Trail ends; turn left and follow arrows.

11.6 Cross Highway 13 and return to parking area.

conjures up an image of life on this rolling prairie. Because it was so difficult to travel overland through the dense hardwood forests, Indians used the Cannon as a watery link between central Minnesota and Wisconsin.

As happened elsewhere in Minnesota, the railroads abandoned many routes to smaller towns that had played a large role in settling this area in the late 1800s. But the misfortune of one group became the fortune of another, as cyclists benefited from these nearly flat corridors being paved. This ride uses part of such a trail, the Sakatah Singing Hills Trail, to avoid the heavy traffic and narrow shoulder of Highway 60.

The Sakatah Lake Loop starts in the former railroad town of Waterville. After riding a short section on Highway 13, turn right at 0.7 mile onto CR 131. For most of the next 6 miles, the road hugs the lakeshore. A thick screen of trees and shrubs is the only barrier that occasionally blocks your view of water. Otherwise, you'll enjoy excellent views of the lake, set against a background of dense hardwood forest.

The pavement of the first 2.4 miles is choppy in spots, but a

30-mph speed limit makes it seem as if you're riding on a quiet lakeside street. At 3.1 miles you cross from LeSueur to Rice County and face a dramatic change in the pavement. Paved within the past few years, this stretch seems to beg riders to pick up the pace on its smooth and nearly seamless surface.

After it crosses a short bridge that separates the upper and lower lakes, the road curves away from water and forms a border between forest and farm fields. At 6.6 miles, after a sharp right curve, turn right onto Sakatah State Trail. Thick foliage hides the trail, so watch for it.

For the first 2 miles of the journey back to town, the trail runs through farmland and prairie. Upon reaching the shore of the lake, you'll enter a tunnel of green formed by oak, elm, walnut, and other hardwoods. If you're wearing dark-tinted sunglasses, you may have to remove them when you enter the forest.

As you ride along the lake, be sure to look left along the ridge that rises above the trail. You'll see several small ravines, at least one of which has a small stream, and brilliant green broadleaf plants that carpet the dark brown forest floor. At 11.5 miles you'll emerge from the canopy, 1 block from the parking area.

The Afton Loop

Distance:	18.1 miles
Approximate Pedaling Time:	2 to 2.5 hours
Terrain:	Hilly, with two mile-long climbs
Traffic:	Light
Surface:	Smooth asphalt
Things to See:	Thick hardwood forests, farms, historic river town, Afton State Park, St. Croix River
Facilities:	Outhouse and drinking water at Afton town park, coffee shop; ice cream parlor, and restaurants in town; restrooms and water at Afton State Park

If you decide to pedal the Afton Loop, you may want to resist the temptation to partake of an ice cream cone from Selma's until after the ride. Although it's difficult to forgo the tasty treats of this quaint ice cream parlor, your stomach will thank you halfway up the coulee climb. And it's always helpful to have an extra incentive at the end of a ride.

Beginning from the historic river town of Afton, this scenic route winds through the spectacular St. Croix River Valley, a National Scenic Waterway. You'll ride well-maintained roads in Washington County, an area caught in the middle of the battle between the quiet rural life and the hustle of the city. One amazing feature of this loop is the sense of isolation you'll often feel, even though you're only fifteen minutes from one of the busiest suburbs in the Twin Cities. The steep forested hillsides, deep cool ravines, and excellent roads make this a favorite ride for many cyclists.

The loop begins in the town park, under the soothing shade

of a stand of stately maple trees. Cyclists can thank the residents of Afton for the beautiful scenery along the first 4 miles of the loop. The county wanted to straighten the road and remove hundreds of trees, but residents fought vehemently until they won. About a quarter-mile into the ride, you'll begin climbing out of the valley. Take your time and try to relax, because this first climb is about 1 mile long. The road curves gently, so instead of having one long climb before you it's broken into three sections.

Upon reaching the top, you'll face a long, gradual descent through an increasingly narrow tunnel of trees. The gentle downhill is the perfect place to get aerodynamic or maybe relax and enjoy the break from climbing. After a short, fast final drop, you'll begin the second ascent. Snaking left and then right, this hill starts steep and stays that way until a few tenths of a mile from the top. As before, relax and perhaps repeat a mantra such as "Climbing is fun." Congratulate yourself on top, since this is the last of the long climbs—the rest are much shorter.

At the crest turn right onto CR 20 heading west, and enjoy the two short descents. The road undulates through lush fields of corn and alfalfa and past prosperous farms. While suburbia hasn't encroached this far yet, the neat farms you're passing may disappear in another generation.

After riding west for about 2.2 miles on CR 20, you will turn right onto CR 71. This road runs straight north for just over 6 miles without even a gentle curve, and it has several challenging climbs. If you're fortunate enough to have a south wind, you'll enjoy the push it provides as you pedal along this smooth road through rolling farmland.

The third intersection takes you along a short section of freeway frontage road; the only ugly part of the loop. A half-mile later you'll turn right on Indian Trail—the epitome of a perfect cycling road—and dive back into the woods. This sweet residential lane twists mostly downhill on smooth, nearly new pavement before merging with CR 21, which leads back to the town of Afton.

Although this loop takes you through the St. Croix River Val-

Ride 10: The Afton Loop

To Minneapolis–St. Paul

Minnesota

HUDSON

Wisconsin

94

Frontage Rd.

Indian Trail

21

95

St. Croix River

NORTH

95

START
AFTON

71

21

Afton State Park

20

Getting There

From St. Paul or Minneapolis, take I–94 east to Highway 95 south. Follow Highway 95 about 3 miles to Afton; park anywhere along the streets bordering the park.

DIREC-TIONS at a glance

0.0 Start at Afton town park, riding south on CR 21.

3.9 Turn right onto CR 20.

6.1 Turn right onto CR 71.

12.8 Turn right onto Frontage Road.

13.3 Turn right onto Indian Trail.

15.6 Turn right onto CR 21.

17.7 Turn right at intersection with Highway 95, which CR 21 merges with for 0.25 mile.

18.1 Arrive back at Afton.

ley, the dense hardwood forest doesn't allow river views, even from the crests of hills. But don't be disappointed about not seeing water. The rugged terrain is prime wildlife habitat, and you may see deer, hawks, or even a reclusive wild turkey. And if you ride this loop in the autumn, you'll cycle through tunnels of red, yellow, and orange as the trees show off their most brilliant colors.

As with most road rides, a weekend morning is the best time to go. You'll be riding well before most people are out, and during the summer you'll beat the heat and often the wind. Before the ride you may want to stop at the small coffee shop in Afton. Sitting on the cobblestone sidewalk sipping a strong cup of coffee evokes feelings of what it's like to cycle Europe.

Once you've completed the loop, you've earned an ice cream cone at Selma's. Located on the site of a Civil War arsenal, this unique shop dishes out some of the best treats around. The selection includes many interesting yet not overly exotic offerings. The ideal way to end your excursion is to grab a treat, walk across the road to the park, and relax in the shade of those majestic maples. After all, you've already burned the calories you're about to consume.

Afton State Park option

At the intersection of CR 21 and CR 20, you can turn left for a scenic side trip into Afton State Park to sample 4 miles of paved trails that take you down to the St. Croix River. When you leave the park, you have two options. For a shorter version of the entire loop and to descend what you just climbed, turn right onto CR 21 upon leaving the park and retrace the route back to Afton. Just make sure your brakes work. To continue the main loop, go straight as you depart the park; doing so will put you on CR 20 heading west.

Stillwater–Withrow Loop

Distance:	19.7 miles
Approximate Pedaling Time:	1.5 to 3 hours
Terrain:	Rolling
Traffic:	Mostly light
Surface:	Smooth asphalt
Things to See:	Thick hardwood forests, farms, lively and vibrant river town; Pioneer Park in Stillwater offers beautiful views of downtown and the St. Croix River.
Facilities:	Stillwater is the largest town on the St. Croix River and has numerous restaurants, shops, and convenience stores. Pine Point Park has restrooms and cold water.

This loop starts at Pine Point, a quiet park about 5 miles north of the bustling St. Croix River town of Stillwater. As the northern terminus of the Gateway Trail, Pine Point sees lots of use from cyclists, in-line skaters, and roller skiers. Long-range plans call for the trail to eventually hook up with the Munger Trail, about 65 miles north. If this dream becomes a reality, a person could ride 150 miles from St. Paul to Duluth on a single paved trail.

Begin the loop by turning right onto CR 55, which goes to Stillwater. A paved bike path parallels the road for a little over a mile before ending, but from this point the road has a shoulder. This stretch of the loop features two hills that come at you in quick succession; although they're not especially difficult, they will test your legs if you're not a climber.

At 4.7 miles turn right onto Myrtle Street, which is CR 12. A

left onto Myrtle will take you down a steep hill to downtown Stillwater and the St. Croix River. This can make a great side trip, but take heed: What goes down must go up, and "up" in this case is a steep climb straight out of the river valley. It's a great and challenging climb, but if you don't like riding up big hills, drive downtown after your ride.

CR 12 is smooth asphalt with full-width shoulders and a paved bicycle path. It's not as quiet as other Washington County roads, but riders will still find themselves surrounded by gently rolling hills and lush farm fields. Soon after leaving town, you'll face a moderate climb about a quarter-mile long. After cresting this hill, the road gradually descends, providing pleasant views of the surrounding country and a temporary break for weary legs until the next climb. The next hill comes at about 8 miles, and it's one of those that never seem to end. It does, but not until you've reached a false summit and pedaled another quarter-mile or so beyond the main pitch.

At 9.8 miles turn right onto CR 9. For the first 2 miles, the road has a wide shoulder and is flat except for a short dip in the landscape. The next 4 miles don't have a shoulder, but traffic is usually light. This section of road rolls over some short gentle hills while twisting through a scenic landscape of occasional ponds, forests, and field. You'll stay on CR 9 until it ends in Withrow, a tiny collection of buildings that includes a ballroom, a school, a bar, and a few houses.

At 15.5 miles turn right onto CR 68, one of the best cycling roads in Washington County, if not Minnesota. This beautiful stretch of quiet country road is a sweet blend of smooth pavement; banked, ninety-degree curves; and great scenery. It's one of those roads that draw you into a zone as you slice gracefully through the curves and settle into a smooth cadence on the gradually descending grade. This country lane may cause you to pick up the pace and pretend you're riding in the Tour de France.

Sadly, CR 68 ends at CR 15, where you'll turn right at 17.9 miles. Go 0.1 mile on CR 15 and turn left onto the Gateway Trail, following it for 1.7 miles, back to Pine Point. The flat

Ride 11: Stillwater–Withrow Loop

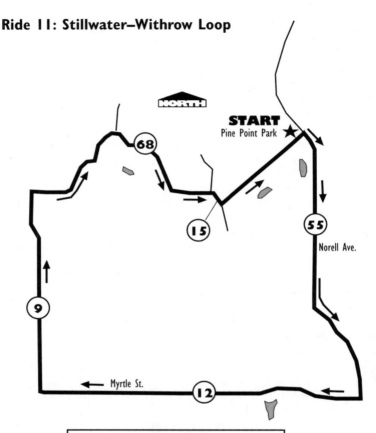

START
Pine Point Park

NORTH

68

15

9

55

Norell Ave.

Myrtle St.

12

Getting There

From St. Paul or Minneapolis, take Highway 96 east to Stillwater. Turn left onto Norell Avenue (CR 55) and follow it for 3 miles to Pine Point Park.

DIRECTIONS at a glance

0.0	Leave park and turn right onto CR 55 (Norell Avenue).
4.7	Turn right onto CR 12 (Myrtle Street).
9.8	Turn right onto CR 9.
15.5	Turn right onto CR 68.
17.9	Turn right onto CR 15.
18.0	Turn left onto the Gateway Trail.
19.7	Return to Pine Point.

grade and thick green canopy of the trail provides a soothing atmosphere for a cool-down spin, especially if you hammered down that last stretch of road. But even if you didn't race your companions, it's still an excellent way to end the ride.

Marine-on-St. Croix Loop

Distance:	22.8 miles
Approximate Pedaling Time:	1.5 to 3 hours
Terrain:	Rolling, with a 0.75-mile-long climb
Traffic:	Light
Surface:	Smooth asphalt
Things to See:	Thick hardwood forests, farms, historic river town, William O'Brien State Park
Facilities:	Outhouse and drinking water at Marine town park; Village Scoop ice cream parlor and restaurants in town. *Note:* Although not located in town, a must stop is Crabtree's Kitchen, 2 miles north in Copas.

This quiet little river settlement is the next-to-last Minnesota town located on the St. Croix River. Similar in size to Afton, it's nestled in a wooded valley 1 mile from scenic William O'Brien State Park. Originally founded as a lumber town, it has become a popular destination for cyclists touring the St. Croix Valley. It's the perfect place to stop for a midride break or to use as a starting point for exploring northern Washington and southern Chisago Counties.

To begin this ride, roll south through town on Judd Street, the quiet main road through town. Cross Highway 95 to CR 7, also known as Nason Hill Road. Like any other road that leaves the river valley, this one climbs. Three-quarters of a mile later, after two moderately steep pitches and a steady climb under a brilliant green canopy of hardwoods, riders emerge to a special treat: A sweet stretch of smooth pavement follows the climb, descending gradually as it winds through more thick forest.

CR 7 climbs a short, moderately steep hill after a sharp left turn and keeps rolling and winding past hobby farms, open fields, and the lush forest lining the river valley. At the next intersection turn right to stay on CR 7, and enjoy the short descent, because it's followed by three more climbs. At this point you're passing Square Lake, which is one of clearest lakes in the region. The park has a swimming beach, a picnic area, restrooms, and water, making it an ideal place for a lunch break.

Continue riding west on CR 7, enjoying the peaceful scenery of northern Washington County. At approximately 8.6 miles you'll arrive at CR 15. Turn right, cross the railroad tracks, and take a quick left onto CR 58. This quiet country lane features smooth pavement and virtually no traffic as it cuts north to CR 57, where you'll turn right. Like most roads in this part of the county, this one rolls past ponds and wide open fields of alfalfa and corn. Look for turtles sunning themselves on logs along ponds, bright white egrets searching for a fish snack, and wild turkey.

After a fun, mile-long straight stretch with several short hills that may tempt you to sprint up them, you'll come to CR 4. Turn right and head east for 8 miles back to Marine. If you have a west wind, you'll have a blast returning, especially since the road descends gradually back to the St. Croix River.

The highlight of the return trip on CR 4 is the final 2 miles, where the descending grade steepens. Gathering speed, you'll plunge deeper into the forest that carpets the valley. Soon after the sky disappears, surrendering to a tunnel of brilliant green, you'll pass under a stone arch bridge. Two hairpin turns guard the underpass, requiring a speed limit for cars of 10 mph through the short maze. Although you can take it faster on a bike, be aware of moisture covering the road under the bridge and cars coming from the other side—factors that may dictate that you don't blast through too fast.

After you clear the bridge, a short straightaway with a couple of tiny rollers will let you and your friends race one another to

Ride 12: Marine-on-St. Croix Loop

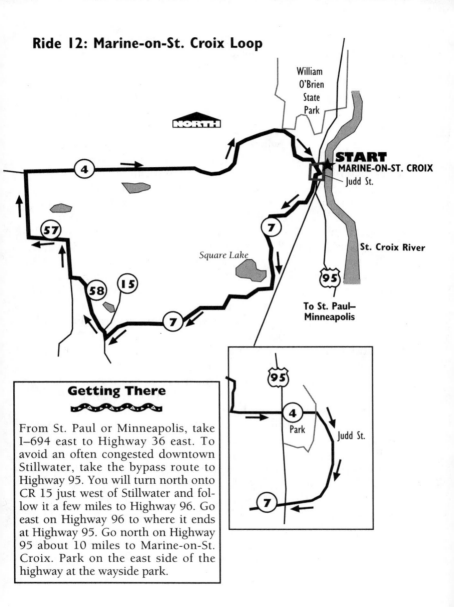

William O'Brien State Park

NORTH

START
MARINE-ON-ST. CROIX
Judd St.

St. Croix River

4

57

58

15

Square Lake

7

7

95

To St. Paul–
Minneapolis

95

4
Park

Judd St.

7

Getting There

From St. Paul or Minneapolis, take I–694 east to Highway 36 east. To avoid an often congested downtown Stillwater, take the bypass route to Highway 95. You will turn north onto CR 15 just west of Stillwater and follow it a few miles to Highway 96. Go east on Highway 96 to where it ends at Highway 95. Go north on Highway 95 about 10 miles to Marine-on-St. Croix. Park on the east side of the highway at the wayside park.

DIREC-TIONS at a glance

0.0 Start at the Marine wayside park, going south on Judd Street.

0.7 Cross Highway 95 to CR 7.

2.3 Turn left onto the paved road, which keeps you on CR 7.

3.8 Turn right to stay on CR 7.

8.6 Turn right onto CR 15 and cross railroad tracks.

8.7 Turn left onto CR 58 (Lynch Road North).

10.7 Turn right onto CR 57.

12.7 Turn right to stay on pavement and CR 57.

14.4 Turn right onto CR 4.

22.2 Turn left to stay on CR 4.

22.8 Arrive back at Marine.

see who buys the after-ride refreshments. At the next intersection turn left and plunge down the hill. As you wind past the church and curve left down the final descent, start feathering the brakes, for a stop sign at the bottom, at Highway 95, sneaks up on unsuspecting riders.

William O'Brien State Park/Crabtree's Kitchen option

For a wonderful side trip from Marine, ride 1.5 miles north on Highway 95 to William O'Brien State Park. Highway 95 has a paved shoulder, and a paved bike path is on the west side of the road. The park has a beautiful swimming beach on the St. Croix and numerous hiking trails if you still have energy after your ride. Another half-mile past the park, you'll find Crabtree's Kitchen, known for awesome breakfasts and incredible pies.

River Road Tour

Distance:	9.9 miles
Approximate Pedaling Time:	1 hour
Terrain:	Mostly flat, with a couple of short hills
Traffic:	Bike path can be busy; roads are moderate
Surface:	Smooth and rough asphalt and concrete
Things to See:	Mississippi River, interesting views of downtown Minneapolis, Ford Dam
Facilities:	Water fountains and restrooms at Minnehaha Park

As the two largest cities in Minnesota, St. Paul and Minneapolis owe much of their existence to the Mississippi River. Derived from the Chippewa name *Messipi,* which means "Father of Waters," the brawny river forms a border between the Twin Cities and is an important commercial and recreational waterway. Whatever the use, however, the two cities have formed an inextricable bond with the Mississippi.

After years of use—and some would argue, abuse—by various industries, both cities are attempting to clean up and change the character of the river on its journey through the area. Gone are the junkyards and ugly concrete highways that in some places occupied space at the river's edge, replaced with bike paths and corridors of green. Though the transformation is not complete and the waterway won't return to its natural state, it's a gradual process that benefits us all.

If you don't have a boat, the next best way to enjoy the

Ride 13: River Road Tour

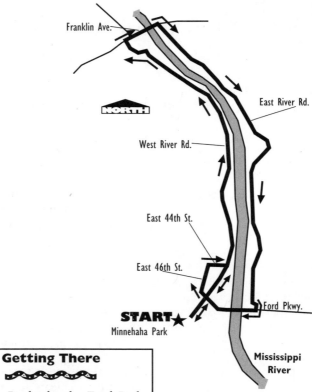

Franklin Ave.

East River Rd.

NORTH

West River Rd.

East 44th St.

East 46th St.

Ford Pkwy.

START ★
Minnehaha Park

Mississippi River

Getting There

From St. Paul take the Ford Parkway Bridge across the Mississippi, take the first left after crossing the river, turn right at the stop sign, and park in any lot along Godfrey Road. From Minneapolis take Highway 55 (Hiawatha Boulevard) to Godfrey Road. Park is on the corner.

DIREC-TIONS at a glance

0.0 Turn right from parking lot and follow the bike trail to West River Road.

3.8 Turn left, following trail across West River Road to eastbound Franklin Avenue.

3.9 Turn right onto Franklin Avenue.

4.1 Turn right onto East River Road.

8.4 Turn left across East River Road and right onto Ford Parkway.

8.9 Turn right onto East 46th Street.

9.3 Turn right onto East 44th Street to West River Road and trail.

9.9 Return to parking lot.

scenery of the river is from the seat of a bicycle. And one of the best trips for a cyclist is on the parkways that wind along the top of the bluffs in St. Paul and Minneapolis. A visit to the river road on any warm summer day will confirm the affinity that city residents have for the great river. You'll see cyclists, in-line skaters, runners, and walkers should you venture to this scenic watery corridor.

From Minnehaha Park follow the paved path northeast under the Ford Parkway Bridge, which will take you along West River Road. It won't take long to deduce why this is some of the best real estate in the Twin Cities. And though riding this loop in the spring or summer provides soothing vistas of this deep, green valley, a special treat awaits if you do it when the trees explode into multicolored hues.

At 0.4 mile you'll pass the visitors' area for the Ford Dam, which supplies power to the Ford Assembly Plant that sits on the east side of the river. Although the thick foliage screens the river from view along much of the trail, you'll find benches placed where the trees thin enough to allow for a glimpse of the water below.

This trail is one of the busiest in the area, especially on weekends, so it's a good idea to relax and slow the pace down a notch or two if you like to ride fast. If ever there was a ride that made slowing down easy to do, this is it. At 3.8 miles turn left across West River Road, and at the top of the hill turn right onto Franklin Avenue to cross the river. Turn right at 4.1 miles onto East River Road. To avoid riding on a street, you can stay on the narrow and rough concrete sidewalk for the next mile.

At 5.1 miles the sidewalk changes to a wider paved path, and it winds around the many small ravines that drop to the river. Compared with the west side of the valley, the east side has more open areas, and these provide spectacular views of the Mississippi and the Minneapolis skyline. You'll also climb more on this side, but the hills are short and gentle.

At 8.4 miles turn left across the road to Ford Parkway and turn right to cross back over the river. Turn right onto East 46th Street at 8.9 miles, and right onto East 44th Street at 9.3 miles, followed by a quick right a few yards later on West River Road. At this point you can ride either the road or the trail back to the park.

Lilydale Park Trail

Distance:	14.0 miles out-and-back
Approximate Pedaling Time:	1 to 2 hours
Terrain:	Flat
Traffic:	None on trail; light on park road
Surface:	Smooth asphalt
Things to See:	Thick hardwood forests, river bluffs, Mississippi River, beautiful views of downtown St. Paul skyline, riverside park on Harriet Island
Facilities:	Outhouses along the trail, Axel's Restaurant (for a great lunch) in town of Mendota along the trail, No Wake Cafe (a houseboat) at Harriet Island

I must confess that I'm not an enthusiastic user of paved recreation trails. Since I usually prefer riding fast, I find them too crowded for my purposes. I do believe, however, that they serve a valuable use as places where families can cycle together, in-line skaters and roller skiers can cruise along, and runners can train without the hassle of motor vehicle traffic.

Despite my bias, the Lilydale Park Trail that runs along the Mississippi and Minnesota Rivers from downtown St. Paul to suburban Eagan impressed me. The western half of this trail is wide, has a yellow line painted down the center, has a white line painted down each side to mark narrow shoulders, and is incredibly smooth asphalt. Compared with other recreational trails, this one ranks as one of the best in the state. According to one rider who uses it frequently, the trail doesn't get crowded, even on weekends. So don't tell too many of your friends.

The trail begins on Harriet Island. As you look across the Mississippi you'll see downtown St. Paul sitting grandly on a bluff about 100 feet above the river. Looking up at the city across the river makes the buildings seem even taller, giving them an almost mystic, Gotham-like quality. Looking farther east, you can see the Mounds Park bluffs, an area of Indian burial mounds that overlook the broad river valley. The ribbon of black runs east to west, following the broad shoulders of the river.

For the first 3 miles, the trail meanders to within yards of the river, switches to a lightly traveled road for two short sections (one smooth, one rough), and crosses under the impressive span of the High Bridge. Although you'll see a few ugly sights, such as a power plant across the river and a few piles of bare dirt, most of this ride features the impressive scenery of the Mississippi and Minnesota River Valleys. If you decide to ride this trail after a heavy rain, beware of dirt on the pavement and one huge but ridable puddle at about 1.3 miles.

As you pedal along the trail, it's easy to see and feel the power of this mighty waterway. Watching the occasional tugboat move a string of barges upstream against the strong current adds to the aura of strength that pulses through the Mississippi. Trees transformed into driftwood lie on sand beaches, left by the river as children's toys scattered around a backyard.

The second half of the trail is newer and provides riders with a greater sense of isolation than the first half. Several historical markers give brief explanations of life in the valley before white settlers arrived in the 1800s. It's fun to imagine how pristine this area must have been 150 years ago.

The trail hugs a narrow strip of riverbank with sandstone bluffs rising steeply up the south side. Although condominiums line the top of the bluff, they're virtually invisible from below. And because this is Minnesota and the trail is in a river valley, lush vegetation lines most of the route.

The Lilydale Park Trail ends at 7.0 miles at a scenic wayside that overlooks the valley, with the international airport across the river. If the winds are blowing right and you love to watch

Ride 14: Lilydale Park Trail

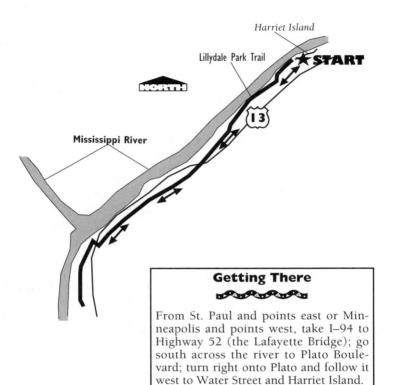

Harriet Island

Lilydale Park Trail

★ **START**

NORTH

13

Mississippi River

Getting There

From St. Paul and points east or Minneapolis and points west, take I–94 to Highway 52 (the Lafayette Bridge); go south across the river to Plato Boulevard; turn right onto Plato and follow it west to Water Street and Harriet Island.

DIRECTIONS at a glance

0.0 Start at Harriet Island parking lot.
0.2 Turn right onto bike path.
1.1 Path temporarily ends; stay right along river.
1.3 Back on path.
2.5 Turn right onto road as path temporarily ends again.
3.2 Turn right onto path just after trestle.
6.4 Take right fork and cross Highway 13.
7.0 Path ends at park.

planes, you'll get some incredible views of the big birds as they make their final approach over the valley. Besides these birds, keep an eye out for hawks and songbirds and for the numerous deer that live in the thick forest. To return to Harriet Island, follow the path back.

Gateway Trail

Distance:	16.5 miles one-way from St. Paul to Pine Point Park
Approximate pedaling time:	1 to 2.5 hours one-way
Terrain:	Flat
Traffic:	No motorized traffic, yet can be busy with cyclists and in-line skaters
Surface:	Smooth asphalt
Things to See:	Rolling hills, patchwork of fields and woods, ponds, Phalen Lake Park (has a public beach)
Facilities:	Outhouses along the trail, convenience stores close to trail in several places and in Mahtomedi/Willernie, Dairy Queen in North St. Paul (5.9 miles), water and restrooms at Pine Point Park

The Gateway Trail is an old railroad right-of-way that the state converted into a recreation trail several years ago. It begins minutes from downtown St. Paul and ends in northern Washington County. The trail provides a safe, scenic corridor through Ramsey County—the most urban county in Minnesota—to a peaceful rural area that seems as if it's 100 miles from the city.

On weekends the Gateway gets crowded with cyclists, in-line skaters, runners, and walkers. If you plan to ride during a weekend and you like to go fast, you may want to ride early or late in the day and bring an extra dose of patience. But if you ride at a slower pace or possess plenty of patience, you probably don't

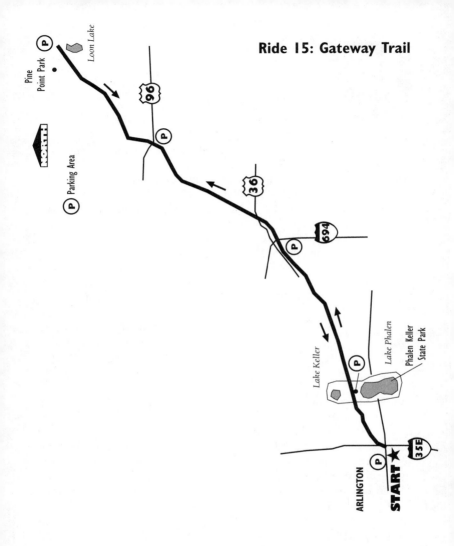

Ride 15: Gateway Trail

Loon Lake

Pine
Point Park

P

96

P

NORTH

P Parking Area

36

694

P

Lake Keller

P

Lake Phalen

Phalen Keller
State Park

35E

P

ARLINGTON

START ★

DIREC-TIONS at a glance

0.0 Start at Arlington trailhead.
1.6 Round Lake Picnic Area in Phalen-Keller Park.
2.5 Trail intersection; continue straight.
3.6 Maplewood Community Center—another good place to start a ride.
7.0 Oakdale trailhead.
10.1 CR 12 crossing.
16.5 End at Pine Point Park.

Getting There

Arlington trailhead: From downtown St. Paul go north on I–35E to the Wheelock Parkway–Larpenteur Avenue exit. Turn right onto Wheelock, go 1 block, and turn right onto Westminster. Follow Westminster for several blocks to Arlington, turn right, and the trailhead is immediately on your left.

Round Lake trailhead: From downtown St. Paul go north on I–35E to the Wheelock Parkway–Larpenteur Avenue exit. Turn right onto Larpenteur and follow it about 0.75 mile to Parkway Drive. Turn left onto Parkway Drive and follow it about 0.5 mile to the Round Lake Picnic Area, which is on your right. To get to the Gateway, follow the trail out of the parking lot, cross the creek, turn left, and follow the trail about 0.1 mile. After going under an arch bridge, look for a path on the right that goes up a short hill. This takes you to the main trail.

Oakdale trailhead: From St. Paul go north on I–35E to Highway 36 east and go east through North St. Paul. One mile east of Century Avenue turn right onto 55th Street and follow it to the trailhead. This trailhead shortens the one-way mileage to 9.5 miles and eliminates numerous street crossings and urban sights.

need to heed that advice. Just go and enjoy the smooth pavement and freedom from motorized vehicles.

Although you won't reach a true rural setting until you've pedaled 7 miles, it's amazing how isolated from the frenetic pace of the city the trail is through Ramsey County. Railroad beds seem to have a mysterious air about them, perhaps because they've occupied thin strips of land that have remained mostly hidden even in the most urban landscapes. Converting these former corridors of powerful machines into recreational paths has softened their industrial features, while retaining the sense of isolation in the midst of organized chaos.

Route finding on the trail is extremely easy; simply follow the trail as it gently curves in a continuous black ribbon from east St. Paul. The trail crosses many streets and roads, spanning the busiest ones with bridges. At 1.6 miles you'll pass along the northern edge of Lake Phalen Park. Paved paths circle Phalen and Round Lakes, and you'll find a large picnic area on the west side of Phalen. Cars do get broken into occasionally at the Arlington trailhead, so you may want to park at the Round Lake picnic area or at the lot at Highway 36 and 55th Street in Oakdale.

After leaving the park and crossing several busy streets through the suburb of North St. Paul, you'll finally reach the last one, at Century Avenue. After crossing Century and paralleling Highway 36 for 1 mile, the trail leaves the busy suburbs behind and enters a much more rural setting. Hobby farms replace city yards, barns replace convenience stores, and road crossings become rarer. As with most state trails, vegetation often forms a canopy that keeps the paths shaded in many areas. Besides the obvious shelter from the sun, the thick rows of trees block the wind (depending on the direction) and lend serenity to the path.

The Gateway Trail passes through progressively more rolling terrain as it cuts northeast. The beauty of a rail trail is that the grade stays nearly constant between 1 and 3 percent. Enjoy the surrounding hills and fact that you won't have to pedal up any of them. At 10 miles the trail crosses CR 12. If you feel the need for caffeine, turn left and follow the bike trail about 0.5 mile to

Willernie. When you enter the tiny downtown, look for the Coffee Cottage on your left.

At 16.5 miles the trail ends at Pine Point Park. This outpost has cold drinking water and real restrooms. It's also a starting point for cyclists exploring northern Washington County. Although it doesn't have much for facilities, it's a great place to relax and refuel before returning to the city.

Options

Numerous loop options exist in Washington County by using the trail and county roads. See Stillwater–Withrow Loop (p. 51) for one option that incorporates the trail with roads.

Farms, Forest, and River Loop

Distance:	25.0 miles
Approximate Pedaling Time:	1.5 to 3.5 hours
Terrain:	Rolling, with a gentle climb from river valley
Traffic:	Light
Surface:	Mostly smooth asphalt, with a couple of moderately rough sections
Things to See:	Thick hardwood forests along the St. Croix River, farms, historic river town, Interstate and Wild River State Parks, Wild Mountain Water Park
Facilities:	Several restaurants in Taylors Falls (including Coffee Talk, Schooney's Soda Shop, and Chisago House), motels, and shops

This scenic ride starts in the small valley town of Taylors Falls, which sits at the head of the highest and steepest cliffs along the St. Croix River. Many years ago this section of the river became known as the Dalles of the St. Croix. Some of the lava cliffs in this Midwest gorge tower as high as 200 feet over the river, while in places the water depth reaches 100 feet. Settled in 1838, the town became an important lumbering center during its early years.

Besides being a historic river town, Taylors Falls sits between two state parks and is a popular destination for rock climbers and canoeists. Almost any road from town climbs steeply—except for the one that you'll ride on this loop. It's a long climb out

Ride 16: Farms, Forest, and River Loop

Getting There

From St. Paul or Minneapolis, take I–35 north to Highway 8 east and follow it for about 25 miles to Taylors Falls. Turn left into town onto Bench Street (Highway 95), go a couple of blocks, and look for the town parking lot on your left.

Alternate route: Follow directions to Marine-on-St. Croix from the Marine-on-St. Croix Loop (p. 56), and follow Highway 95 north for 15 miles, to Highway 8 east. This section of Highway 95 is a beautiful drive.

DIREC-TIONS at a glance

0.0	Start at the town parking lot on Bench Street by going north.
0.3	Turn right onto CR 16.
11.1	Turn left onto CR 12.
11.7	Cross Highway 95 and continue on CR 12.
16.3	Turn left onto CR 20.
23.7	Turn right to stay on CR 20.
24.4	Turn left to stay on CR 20.
24.8	Turn left onto Bench Street.
25.0	Arrive at parking lot.

of the valley, yet several level stretches make it more pleasant than a continual ascent.

Starting in the clean and compact downtown, the route follows Bench Street (Highway 95) just 0.3 mile before turning onto CR 16. While it's possible to continue on Highway 95, it gets busy, especially on weekends, and the county road is much quieter. At about 6.7 miles you'll come to Wild Mountain. A ski area during the winter, Wild Mountain operates a water park during the summer. Although it's probably too early in your ride to stop for a soak, you might want to return later.

CR 16 climbs along the river in steps, none of which is particularly long or steep. The scenery on this part of the loop alternates between tunnels of green that shade riders from the sun and small fields shared by cows, horses, and, often, deer. Although you will occasionally see the St. Croix, the thick forest of maple and pine will screen it much of the time. As you climb out of the valley, watch for hawks riding air currents above the river and for reclusive wild turkeys cautiously feeding along the edges of pastures.

At the intersection with CR 12, turn left and follow it through the tiny town of Almelund. A right turn onto CR 12 will take you to Wild River State Park, a good postride stop. This road isn't the most scenic part of the ride, but you're on it for only 4 miles. It's a pleasant, flat country road, and a few more houses are along it. The real treat awaits on CR 20.

After turning left onto CR 20, you'll see a ridge forming a green horizon in the distance, which is the Wisconsin side of the St. Croix River Valley. This smooth section of road descends gradually, almost to the point where you know the pedaling just got easier but are unsure why. The farms you'll pass on this road tend to be smaller dairy operations, instead of the large crop and livestock ones that are common in western Minnesota. The fields are small and are wedged between dense stands of forest and numerous wetlands. As you cruise through the peaceful countryside, the Wisconsin hills will seem to draw you back toward town.

After seven outstanding and fun miles, you'll arrive in town. Several turns and one rough but short stretch of pavement later, you're back in downtown Taylors Falls, energized by the final descents for an afternoon of hiking, canoeing, or soaking at the water park.

Minnehaha Creek to Lake Harriet

Distance:	11.2 miles out and back or 20.9 with Three Lake Loop
Approximate Pedaling Time:	1 to 3 hours
Terrain:	Mostly flat, with a couple of short hills
Traffic:	No motorized vehicles; busy with cyclists and in-line skaters
Surface:	Rough asphalt
Things to See:	Minnehaha Creek and Falls, interesting views of downtown, Lake Nokomis (has beach), Lake Hiawatha
Facilities:	Water fountains and restrooms along route at lakes, refreshment stands at beaches

Appropriately called the City of Lakes, Minnesota's largest city can trace much of its history to an association with water. Minneapolis, whose name combines the Indian word for "water" (*minne*) with the Greek word for "city" (*polis*), had origins as a sawmill and flour mill for the soldiers at nearby Fort Snelling. First known as St. Anthony for the falls on the Mississippi River, the small village merged with a neighboring town and grew into a major lumber- and flour-milling center.

This ride begins at Minnehaha Park, which sits on the creek of the same name. Minnehaha Falls is a prominent feature of the park, and hiking trails follow the creek a short distance to its junction with the Mississippi. It's well worth the time to hike around the area after finishing a ride. Minnehaha Falls is the

Ride 17: Minnehaha Creek to Lake Harriet

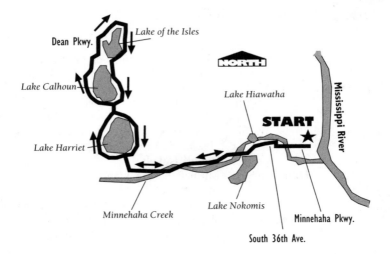

Dean Pkwy.

Lake of the Isles

Lake Calhoun

Lake Harriet

NORTH

Lake Hiawatha

START

Mississippi River

Minnehaha Creek

Lake Nokomis

Minnehaha Pkwy.

South 36th Ave.

Getting There

From St. Paul take the Ford Parkway Bridge across the Mississippi; take the first left after crossing the river; turn right at the stop sign and park in any lot along Godfrey Road. From Minneapolis take Highway 55 (Hiawatha Boulevard) to Godfrey Road. Park is on the corner.

**DIREC-
TIONS**
at a glance

0.0 Start at Minnehaha Falls parking lot; follow Godfrey Road west.

0.3 Right onto South 36th Avenue.

0.4 Cross East 47th Street (36th Avenue ends here), veer slightly left, and get on sidewalk and follow it across the creek to the main trail.

1.1 Take left fork in trail.

1.5 Take right fork to stay on main trail.

3.2 Trail switches to other side of road.

4.8 Turn left to cross creek.

5.4 Continue straight onto street (has marked bike lane, which may be hard to see).

5.6 Arrive at Lake Harriet; return by the same route for out-and-back.

Three Lakes Loop option:

5.6 Go left on paved path (it's one-way) along Lake Harriet.

7.1 Go left and cross street to get to Lake Calhoun.

9.1 Left at intersection onto Dean Parkway.

9.5 Right to stay on Dean, which goes to Lake of the Isles.

12.1 Left at intersection to return to Lake Calhoun.

13.7 Left at stoplight to return to Lake Harriet.

15.3 Left at intersection to return to Minnehaha Creek Trail.

20.9 Return to Minnehaha Park.

most popular feature of the park, especially after the creek rises following a heavy rain.

Perhaps the most striking aspect of this trail for me is how quiet and calm it was on a Saturday in July. We expected to be constantly dodging other bikes, runners, and in-line skaters. Instead, we cruised along totally unimpeded for much of the ride. As cars and bikes zipped by on the parkway, the path remained

relatively uncrowded. At times it can get more crowded, but for us it stayed remarkably deserted until we reached Lake Harriet.

This out-and-back ride begins at the park, located on Godfrey Road and Minnehaha Avenue. You'll find plenty of parking, it costs $1.00 per day on the honor system, and this location also makes a good place to start the River Road Tour.

From the main picnic area, follow the paved path left to the first stoplight. The path ends temporarily, so follow Minnehaha Parkway (which is Godfrey Road east of the lights) through two intersections. At 0.3 mile, turn right onto South 36th Avenue, and at 0.4 mile, cross East 47th Street and look for a sidewalk that goes toward the creek. Congratulations—you've found the Minnehaha Creek Trail! After the short ride through an urban mess, you're about to enter a scenic corridor through the heart of a densely populated city.

Immediately after merging onto the path, you'll cross the creek and turn left to stay on the main route. The pavement on the trail is rough, which is the only negative aspect about it. I recommend using a mountain or cross (hybrid) bike. You'll have a jarring ride on a road bike, because of numerous cracks in the surface and some rough approaches to bridges that cross the creek.

At 1.1 miles take the left fork in the trail to stay on the main path. As you crest the short grade, look right over Lake Hiawatha for a view of the Minneapolis skyline looming over the lake. At 1.5 miles go right to stay on the main route. A left will take you to a trail that circles Lake Nokomis, the centerpiece of Nokomis Park.

At 3.2 miles the trail crosses Minnehaha Parkway to get back along the creek. After you've been riding in open boulevards for the past few miles, the trail suddenly becomes enveloped by a thick canopy of greenery. The sky temporarily disappears, along with noise from a nearby busy street. At 4.8 miles turn left over the creek, which also keeps you on pavement. At 5.4 miles the trail merges with a residential street, taking riders to the shore of Lake Harriet, at 5.6 miles.

Upon reaching the lake, you can either return to Minnehaha Falls or add 10 miles to the ride by going around the three main lakes that constitute the chain. For another pleasant option, pedal the short loop around Lake Nokomis before returning to the park.

Mille Lacs Lake Loop

Distance:	30.1 miles
Approximate Pedaling Time:	2 to 3.5 hours
Terrain:	Mostly flat, with some rolling terrain
Traffic:	Heavy on Highway 169 (has wide shoulder), light to moderate on Highway 27, light elsewhere
Surface:	Smooth asphalt
Things to See:	Lakes Mille Lacs, Shakopee, and Onamia; Mille Lacs Kathio State Park; Mille Lacs Indian Museum
Facilities:	Restaurants, grocery store in Onamia; resorts with water and snacks along Mille Lacs

When the first human beings stood on the shore of Mille Lacs Lake, they must have stared in awe. The lake is 22 miles long and 14 miles wide, and early settlers and Indians probably felt as if they had stumbled upon an inland sea. The lake was known as Spirit Lake by the Indians; early French explorers called the area *Mille Lacs,* which means "1,000 Lakes." The region features a long, rich history that continues to evolve.

Lured by the bounty of fish and wild rice, people have lived along the lake for 4,000 years. Hundreds of years before the Europeans arrived, the Dakota lived in what is now Mille Lacs Kathio State Park and the tribespeople became known as the *Mdewakanton,* or "Those Who Live by the Water of the Great Spirit." In the eighteenth century the Ojibwe began moving in from the east, and soon thereafter the Dakota left the area.

A great forest of white and red pine originally covered the re-

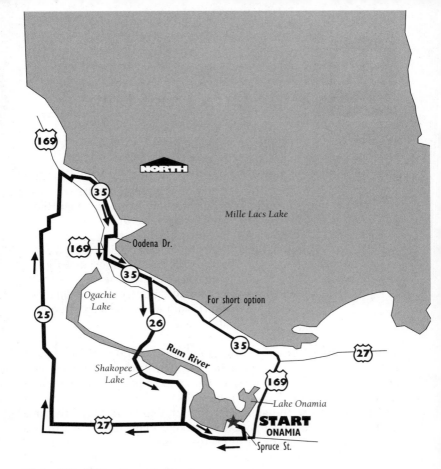

Ride 18: Mille Lacs Lake Loop

Getting There

From the Twin Cities take Highway 169 to Onamia. Follow Highway 27 west through downtown, turn right onto Spruce Street and follow it to the town park.

0.0 Start at Onamia town park (left from park and right on Spruce).

0.3 Turn right onto Main Street (Highway 27).

6.5 Turn right onto CR 25.

15.9 Turn right onto Highway 169.

16.0 Turn left onto CR 35 (be careful crossing Highway169).

18.8 Turn right onto Oodena Drive.

18.8 Turn left onto Highway 169.

20.2 Turn left onto CR 35 (be careful crossing Highway 169).

22.1 Turn right onto CR 26.

28.3 Turn left onto Highway 27.

29.8 Turn left onto Spruce Street.

30.1 Return to town park.

Short option:

0.0 Start at Onamia town park.

0.3 Turn right onto Main Street (Highway 27).

1.8 Turn right onto CR 26.

7.9 Cross Highway 169.

8.0 Turn right onto CR 35.

12.2 Turn left to stay on CR 35.

12.9 Turn right onto Highway 27.

12.9 Turn left onto Highway 169 (narrow shoulder and heavy traffic).

15.5 Turn right onto Highway 27 into Onamia.

16.2 Turn right onto Spruce Street.

16.5 Return to town park.

gion, extending many miles to the south. Logging started in the 1850s, and within fifty years most of the virgin forest had vanished. Today Mille Lacs has become one of the most popular fishing lakes in Minnesota and is best known for walleye, the state fish. Indian life has changed, as the tribe has built a large casino on the south shore to harvest dollars as well as wild rice.

As you leave town on Highway 27, you'll pass Lake Onamia, part of a three-lake chain that, with Mille Lacs, forms the headwaters of the Rum River. Although the highway has a narrow shoulder, light traffic and a smooth surface make it a good cycling road. As you ride along, you'll pass through the quintessential transition landscape of northern Minnesota: massive swamps, patches of mixed forest, and, yes, the ubiquitous farm field.

At 6.5 miles turn onto CR 25 and head north toward the big lake. The minor cracks and bumps in the road serve as a reminder of the freeze-thaw cycle and perpetually damp soil of northern regions. After winding along the west side of the state park, the road teases riders with what's ahead.

While cruising down the last gentle hill toward the lake, you'll notice a patch of blue shining through the corridor of green. You've just caught a first glimpse of Mille Lacs, and soon you'll get to enjoy several miles of stunning lake views. At 15.9 miles turn right onto Highway 169, and follow it with a careful left at 16.0 miles onto CR 35. Although Highway 169 has a wide shoulder along the lake, it carries heavy traffic, an aspect that ruins the solace you should experience near water.

CR 35 provides a front-row view of Minnesota's second largest lake as it hugs the shore. You won't notice it, but you'll be riding on a ridge of debris deposited by glaciers that formed a natural dam.While enjoying the beautiful lake views, you may notice little wooden shacks sitting in front of resorts. After the lake freezes, people pull the structures onto the ice and fish from them. Resorts plow highwaylike roads on the ice and put wooden bridges over the large cracks that always form, and the shacks group together to form small ice towns.

After a short detour onto Highway, 169, turn back onto CR 35 for 2 more miles of lakeshore pedaling. At 22.1 miles turn right onto CR 26, cross Highway 169, and enjoy the next 6 miles of quiet county road. As you pass the state park and Shakopee Lake on the return trip to Onamia, watch for eagles and osprey soaring above the forest.

Lakes of Grand Rapids

Distance:	11.8 miles
Approximate Pedaling Time:	1 to 1.5 hours
Terrain:	Rolling to flat
Traffic:	Moderate on Highway 169, light elsewhere
Surface:	Mostly smooth asphalt, one slightly rough section
Things to See:	Scenic lake country, thick evergreen forest, Morrison and Horseshoe Lakes
Facilities:	Water and outhouses at park, all services in Grand Rapids

As beautiful as the thick evergreen forest around Grand Rapids is today, you have to wonder what it was like several generations ago when a virgin forest of 150-foot-tall white pine covered the region. Visitors can still see the occasional crown of one of these majestic specimens towering above the second- and third-growth forest, a lonely remnant of the vast carpet that once was. The huge trees provided incredible amounts of timber, and the massive stands of red and white pine—probably more trees than most lumberjacks had ever seen—led to the logging version of a gold rush.

Besides being in the middle of the massive northern forests, Grand Rapids also sits among two other significant geographic landmarks: The town perches along the upper reaches of the Mississippi River, at the point past which steamboats could not travel, and lies at the western edge of the Mesabi Iron Range. It's also the birthplace of Judy Garland.

The ride begins in Veterans Memorial Park, which occupies

Ride 19: Lakes of Grand Rapids

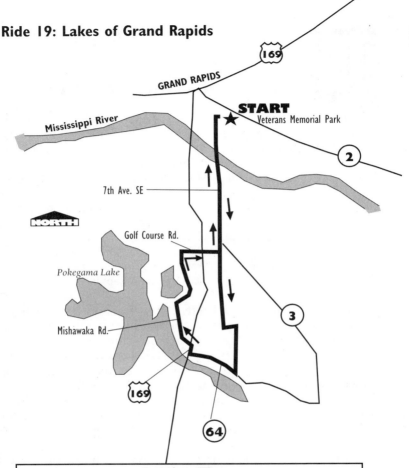

169

GRAND RAPIDS

START
Veterans Memorial Park

Mississippi River

2

7th Ave. SE

NORTH

Golf Course Rd.

Pokegama Lake

3

Mishawaka Rd.

169

64

Getting There

From the Twin Cities take Highway 169 north to Grand Rapids. Or take I–35 north to Moose Lake and Highway 73. Take Highway 73 north to Highway 2 and take 2 west to Grand Rapids. The park is located at the intersection of Highway 2 and 7th Avenue Southeast in the southeast edge of Grand Rapids. It's near the intersection of Highways 2 and 169.

DIREC-TIONS
at a glance

0.0 Turn left onto 7th Avenue Southeast from Veterans Memorial Park.
3.8 Turn right onto CR 64.
6.0 Turn right onto Highway 169.
6.2 Turn left onto Mishawaka Road.
9.8 Turn right onto Golf Course Road.
11.0 Turn left onto 7th Avenue Southeast.
11.8 Return to park.

Option:
0.0 Turn left onto 7th Avenue Southeast from Veterans Memorial Park.
3.8 Turn left onto CR 64.
6.0 Turn left onto CR 3.
10.2 Turn right onto 7th Avenue Southeast.
10.5 Return to park.

the former site of the Swan River Logging Co. From this location workers rolled logs into the Mississippi, the beginning of a 327 mile river journey to sawmills in Minneapolis. Over the years thirty-five million board feet of lumber have floated from this site. Leaving the park turn left onto 7th Avenue Southeast, which for the first mile may be busy as it passes through a commercial and residential area.

By continuing straight at 1.3 miles, you'll enter a much more rural zone of Grand Rapids. Although this road is rough, it's a quiet route, with little traffic and pleasant wooded vistas. You'll face several rolling climbs early on, but eventually the road tilts down before leveling out. It also has two ninety-degree, slightly banked corners to play on.

At 3.8 miles turn right onto CR 64, a wide and nearly flat

road with a smooth surface. This road ends at Highway 169, where you'll turn right at 6.0 miles. At 6.2 miles, a left turn onto Mishawaka Road takes you away from broad county roads and highways to another intimate country lane. With smooth pavement and a thick canopy of trees forming a tunnel of green, you will, before long, forget you just crossed a major highway.

After a short flat stretch, the road heads down a steep hill that suddenly appears without warning. While it's tempting to blast down this hill, watch for vehicles coming out of driveways. But don't worry about that old adage "what goes down . . . ," since you won't face any big climbs. The remaining ascents are short, with gentle grades, and provide enough relief to keep the ride from becoming too easy.

Like other roads in northern lake country, the 3 miles of Mishawaka Road (which becomes Horseshoe Lake Road) is a classic Minnesota lake loop. Most of these scenic routes have smooth pavement, wind through thick forest, and pass the ever present cabins and houses with neatly manicured yards. Even with all the houses, you'll still have some good—albeit quick—lake views.

At 9.8 miles you'll emerge from the serenity of the lakes to turn right onto Golf Course Road. This road has wide shoulders, and even with traffic it's an excellent cycling road. At 11.0 miles turn left onto 7th Avenue Southeast and return to the park. Besides this ride and the option described below, the area has many more paved county roads to explore.

For a different look at the area, turn left onto CR 64 at 3.8 miles. The open roadbeds of CR 64 and CR 3 provide wide-angle views of the surrounding forest instead of the close-up look you had when riding along the lakes. And if you have lots of energy, you can do both loops.

Roaming the Range

Distance:	20.0 miles
Approximate Pedaling Time:	2 hours
Terrain:	Mostly flat, with several rolling hills
Traffic:	Moderate on Highway 169, light elsewhere
Surface:	Mostly smooth asphalt
Things to See:	Hill Annex Mine, Swan Lake, northern forest, Mesabi Iron Range
Facilities:	Restrooms at Hill Annex–Calumet Park, gift shop with ice cream and snacks at the park, convenience store in Calumet

The most remarkable aspect of this ride may be what you see before and after it instead of on it. As you pedal along, you'll see a scenic north woods lake, endless tracts of forest, and piles of reddish iron-ore tailings. But the most spectacular sight—the Hill Annex Mine—sits at the top of the hill where the ride begins and ends. From an observation platform 500 feet above the floor of the huge open pit, you'll have spectacular views of the mine. And just east of Calumet, piles of red rock tower like miniature mountains above Highway 169.

The town lies on the Mesabi Iron Range, once the richest-known source of high-grade iron ore in the world. Like many other mining regions, it has a history of boom and bust. As you roam around the region, you'll see reminders of the mining activity from the past and the present. Thick stands of aspen have reestablished themselves on the massive piles of tailings, helping to reshape much of the landscape into a blend of steep, Appalachian-like hills and deep pits that have filled with cold, clear groundwater. Several years ago entrepreneurs converted some abandoned pits into trout hatcheries.

Although it's not on this ride, Hibbing, located about 18 miles east of Calumet, makes an interesting stop if you're in the area. Besides having a rich mining history, Hibbing was also the childhood home of music legend Bob Dylan and the birthplace of the Greyhound Bus Company. Present-day Hibbing sits 2 miles south of its original location, moved because of the discovery of rich iron ore under the town. Just north of Hibbing a rare three-way continental divide formed. At this point rain falling flows to Hudson Bay, the North Atlantic, and the Gulf of Mexico.

If you can tear yourself away from the mine, you'll ride back through Calumet to Highway 169 and turn left. The highway gets busy at times but has a wide shoulder. As you leave town, if you look left you'll see the huge piles of waste rock from the Hill Annex Mine. At 2.0 miles turn right onto CR 83. You'll enjoy a long, gradual descent almost immediately but will have to climb a short hill soon thereafter. At 4.2 miles, after rounding two sharp curves, turn left onto Highway 65, followed at 4.5 miles with a right onto CR 12, which circles Swan Lake.

You've reached one of the best roads in this area, if not in all of northern Minnesota. Featuring smooth pavement, wide shoulders for the first 4 miles, light traffic, and a 30- to 40-mph speed limit, it's a relaxing stretch of nearly perfect cycling road. Unfortunately, you won't have lake views, but the quality of the surface makes it easy to forget such details and the thick forest on the side opposite the lake provides a scenic background.

At 8.7 miles the shoulder ends, but the pavement stays smooth and the speed limit increases only to 40 mph. With a narrower roadbed, the forest closes in some, giving the route a more intimate feel. At 12.3 miles turn left onto Highway 65, and then right onto CR 12 at 12.5 miles. Although the next 7 miles

Ride 20: Roaming the Range

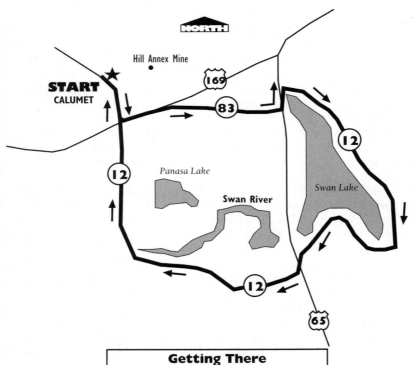

Getting There

From Highway 169 turn onto the main street into Calumet and go up the hill to the Hill Annex–Calumet Park.

**DIREC-
TIONS**
at a glance

0.0 Start at the park and go down the main street to Highway 169.
0.3 Turn left onto Highway 169.
2.0 Turn right onto CR 83.
4.2 Turn left onto Highway 65.
4.5 Turn right onto CR 12.
12.3 Turn left onto Highway 65.
12.5 Turn right onto CR 12.
19.7 Cross Highway 169.
20.0 Return to park.

of road aren't as smooth as the road was around the lake, CR 12 has light traffic as it winds through the dense northern forest. As you near Calumet, you'll start to see a few piles of red rocks from mines that have ceased operating.

At 19.7 miles cross Highway 169 for the short climb back to the park. It's now time to continue staring at the huge mine.

Cruising Along Gitchee Gummi

Distance:	9.6 miles
Approximate Pedaling Time:	1 hour
Terrain:	Flat
Traffic:	Light to moderate
Surface:	Smooth asphalt
Things to See:	Spectacular views of Lake Superior
Facilities:	Outhouses at park, deli and restaurants along CR 61, all services in Duluth

As the largest of the Great Lakes, Lake Superior has played and continues to play an important role in the lives of northern residents. From the first Indians who lived along the rocky north shore, to the voyageurs who plied the icy waters in 36-foot canoes loaded with fur pelts, to the massive ore boats that transport untold tons of taconite pellets from the iron ranges of northern Minnesota, Lake Superior is to the North what the Mississippi is to the South.

Duluth's history dates back to 1679, when French explorer Daniel de Greysolan, Sieur du Luth—whose name eventually graced the city—landed on what is now Minnesota Point. The North West Company established a trading post here in 1792, but it wasn't until 1852 that a permanent settlement sprang up. With the discovery of iron and gold on the Mesabi Iron Range in 1865, Duluth soon became an important port city. As the largest inland port in the world, the city became a principal shipper of not only iron ore but also grain from the Red River Valley and lumber from the vast forests that blanket the region.

Ride 21: Cruising along Gitchee Gummi

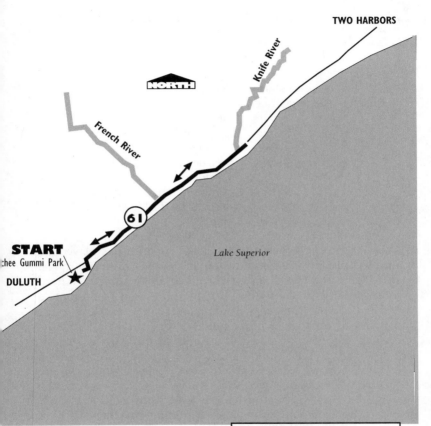

TWO HARBORS

Knife River

NORTH

French River

61

START
chee Gummi Park

DULUTH

Lake Superior

Getting There

From the intersection of I–35 and London Road, go north on London Road 3.7 miles to Gitchee Gummi Park. Park in larger lot in center of park.

DIREC-TIONS at a glance

0.0 Follow park road north (away from town) along the lake.
0.5 Turn right onto CR 61.
4.8 Reach Lakeview Castle restaurant.
9.1 Turn left back to park.
9.6 Return to main lot.

Long ride option:

0.0 Follow park road north (away from town) along the lake.
0.5 Turn right onto CR 61.
4.8 Reach Lakeview Castle restaurant.
12.7 Knife River.
13.1 Emily's Deli.
21.7 Turn left back to park.
26.2 Return to main lot.

Note: To change this route from an out-and-back to a loop, you would have to return to the park along the expressway that connects Duluth with Two Harbors. It wouldn't be a fun return trip.

From beautiful Gitchee Gummi Park, located north of downtown Duluth, ride along the quiet park road 0.5 mile as it closely follows the craggy shore. In a perfect cycling world, this paved lane would run along the lake for many miles; however, in our imperfect world this road ends at CR 61, where you'll turn right. This nearly flat road received a new coat of blacktop recently, giving it the kind of seamless surface that all road cyclists dream of.

As a designated scenic road, CR 61 hugs the shore for 23 miles to Two Harbors. Before receiving this special designation, it was the original Highway 61 that connected New Orleans with Canada. Along this stretch of road, you're seeing the beginning of the North Shore, an area that many Minnesotans revere. Although residents enjoy and visit other parts of Minnesota, especially the lake country that lies farther west, the north shore of Lake Superior has an almost magical effect on many of us.

Though it does get busy at times, CR 61 provides intimate views of the lake and sometimes runs barely 25 yards from the shore. It also has many scenic overlooks with picnic tables, offering perfect places to rest while gazing at the largest lake in the world. As you look across the lake, you'll see the northern Wisconsin shore on the horizon. This is the narrow part of the lake; it gets much wider farther north.

At 4.8 miles you'll reach the appropriately named Lakeview Castle restaurant. For the short ride turn around here and follow the highway back to the park. If you feel like putting on a few more miles, keep riding along the shore. At 6.0 miles you'll reach a little country cafe and at 6.5 miles you'll cross the French River, where you'll find an outhouse and a picnic area.

You'll reach the village of Knife River at 12.7 miles, and soon thereafter, at 13.1 miles, you'll arrive at Emily's Deli. Those who ride a few miles farther will pass the starting line of Grandma's Marathon, a popular running race held in June.

Energetic riders can continue north to Two Harbors, which is the second largest town on the north shore and has many gift shops and cafes. If you plan on riding this far, you may want to make sure you have a north wind to push you back—or keep riding until you reach Canada, 135 miles later.

Touring Tettegouche Country

Distance:	20.2 miles
Approximate Pedaling Time:	3 to 3.5 hours
Terrain:	Hilly
Traffic:	Moderate to heavy on Highway 61, light elsewhere
Surface:	Mostly smooth asphalt
Things to See:	Tettegouche State Park, spectacular views of Lake Superior and the vast northern forest
Facilities:	Restrooms and water at the state park, convenience store in Finland

When we think of volcanic activity, it's usually associated with the Pacific Rim or someplace with spectacular volcanoes jutting above the landscape. Most of us don't normally think of Minnesota as being located in a region of such activity. But about 1.1 billion years ago, North America began to spread apart along a rift from what became Lake Superior to Kansas. The lava that flowed from this crack eventually tilted toward the lake and formed the Sawtooth Mountains. After these Midwest mountains rose from the lake, glacial meltwater slowly gnawed through the rock to form the many waterfalls and spectacular canyons that mark the North Shore landscape.

The forest in this area also has some unique aspects. Much of forest along this ride consists of a boreal, or northern, forest. Since the thin rocky soils, long cold winters, and short warm summers exclude many varieties of plants, only species that tolerate such conditions survive. Along the north shore, trees well

suited to this climate include birch, aspen, and spruce.

But another tree, the maple, survives in temperate microclimates on the ridges above the lake. During the winter, when subzero temperatures cover the region, air from a warmer Lake Superior protects the maples. And during the summer, when cool breezes blow off the lake, warm winds from inland caress the trees along the ridges and help extend the growing season. Although beautiful during the summer, the maples show off their best in the fall, when they turn a brilliant red.

If you don't like to climb, you may want to skip this ride, or perhaps drive it to take in the exceptional scenery. But if you like climbing, you'll love this road. After leaving Tettegouche and warming up with a gentle climb on Highway 61, turn left onto Highway 1 at 0.6 mile. The road rears up immediately, climbing away from the big lake for 1.3 miles. You'll get a short break before beginning another ascent at 2.1 miles, a climb that lasts about a mile. Soon thereafter you'll start another 1.3-mile climb, which brings the total uphill mileage to nearly 4 miles.

If you ride this road during autumn, the maples will provide a color show that may make you forget the long uphill ride. After a fun descent into the village of Finland, turn right onto CR 6 at 6.6 miles. Try not to cry after crossing the Baptism River, because you'll now go up the ridge you just flew down. Life (and cycling) isn't always fair.

This quiet road winds through a classic northern landscape, with an occasional white pine from the virgin forest dominating the landscape. You'll pass through lush wetlands that sit below imposing rock faces. As the road rolls back to the lake, notice how the Sawtooths tilt up at a gentle angle on one side before ending in a vertical wall. And try to imagine how far to the north this forest reaches.

At 12 miles you'll finally receive your reward for all the climbing: After you've soaked in an incredible vista of Lake Superior, the road tilts down; at 13 miles the road swoops left for a final steep approach to the shore and gives you the feeling of falling into the lake.

Ride 22: Touring Tettegouche Country

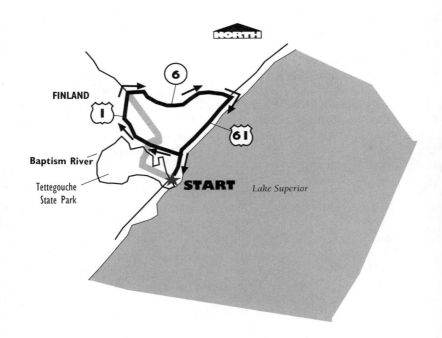

Getting There

Follow Highway 61 about 34 miles north of Two Harbors to Tettegouche State Park and Wayside. Park in the rest area lot.

DIREC-TIONS at a glance

0.0	From parking lot turn right onto Highway 61.
0.6	Turn left onto Highway 1.
6.6	Turn right onto CR 6.
13.7	Turn right onto Highway 61.
16.3	Shoulder gets much wider.
20.2	Turn left and return to park.

Short option:

0.0	From parking lot turn right onto Highway 61.
0.6	Turn left onto Highway 1.
6.6	Arrive in Finland and go back the way you came.
12.6	Turn right onto Highway 61.
13.2	Turn left and return to park.

Note: For riders not comfortable cycling along the narrow section of Highway 61, this out-and-back provides an alternative. Of course, you still have to climb.

You'll turn right onto Highway 61 at 13.7 miles and face the only bad part of the loop. Although the highway has a narrow shoulder for the next 2.5 miles, it carries heavy traffic at times. At 16.3 miles the shoulder gets wider, but much bumpier. Still, it's a fair trade for the final 4 rolling miles back to the park, which end with a slight downhill. I guess life is fair after all.

Route of the Voyageurs

Distance:	22.1 miles
Approximate Pedaling Time:	2 to 3 hours
Terrain:	Rolling to hilly
Traffic:	Light to moderate
Surface:	Asphalt and short stretches of gravel
Things to See:	Grand Portage National Monument, spectacular views of Lake Superior
Facilities:	Restrooms at monument, convenience store a quarter-mile away

Grand Portage, the "Great Carrying Place," played an important role in the history of this region. Used for many years by the Cree and Ojibwa, who lived in the area, the Grand Portage provided an overland route from the more tranquil waters of the upper Pigeon River to Lake Superior. The tribes used this portage to avoid the rapids and waterfalls on the lower river and to reach the quiet waters that allowed them to canoe deep into the heart of the wilderness forming the border between the United States and Canada. Today this massive network of lakes comprises the Boundary Waters Canoe Area and Quetico Provincial Park.

In the mid-1600s French explorers known as voyageurs arrived and thus began a new era in the north woods. Soon thereafter, fueled by an insatiable demand for furs in Europe and what seemed like an infinite supply of beaver, trappers started venturing ever deeper into Canada, searching for pelts. In 1784 Grand Portage became the headquarters of the North West Company, as well as an important rendezvous for the north men (winterers) who plied the wilderness for furs and the Montreal men (porkeaters) who took the pelts east through the Great Lakes.

Ride 23: Route of the Voyageurs

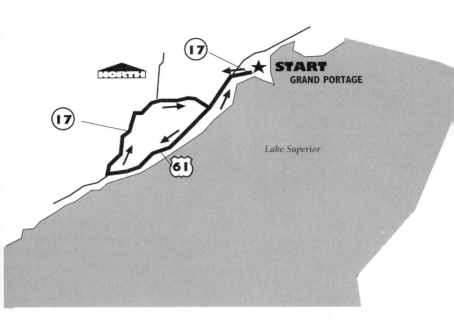

Getting There

Follow Highway 61 36 miles north of Grand Marais, turn right onto CR 17, and go 1 mile to the monument.

DIREC-TIONS at a glance

0.0 From parking lot turn left onto CR 17.
1.0 Turn left onto Highway 6.1
10.2 Turn right onto CR 17.
16.5 Turn right to stay on CR 17.
20.5 Turn left onto Highway 61.
21.1 Turn right onto CR 17.
22.1 Return to monument lot.

Held in July, Rendezvous became an important business and social time for voyageurs, company partners, and clerks. The portage remained a significant link between northwestern Canada and Montreal until 1803. As you wander around the old fort, try to imagine hundreds of voyageurs camped along the shore, celebrating with the company men from Montreal.

To begin the ride, turn left onto CR 17 from the parking lot and follow it 1 mile to Highway 61. You'll turn left onto Highway 61 and follow it along the shore for the next 9 miles. The highway has a wide shoulder, and the sometimes rough pavement improves dramatically at 5.9 miles. As you pedal along the gently rolling road, you'll have a mixture of North Shore scenery. The road passes through thick stands of birch and aspen and then bursts out of the forest to spectacular views of Lake Superior or the ridges of the Sawtooth Mountains.

At 10.2 miles you'll turn right onto a poorly marked CR 17, which is the old Highway 61. Upon turning onto the county road, you'll go from a highway recently reborn to one that is slowly dying. After pedaling along on a smooth surface, you'll climb the tall ridge on cracked blacktop pitted with potholes. Instead of trying to resurface the road, the county now fills in the worst spots with gravel. In ten years CR 17 may be more gravel than asphalt.

Because of the rough pavement and patches of gravel, I recommend using a mountain, cross, or touring bike. After reaching the top of the ridge, the road drops gradually, providing beautiful views of the vast forest. At 16.5 miles turn right to stay on CR 17. At this point you'll leave the past and return to the present as the road becomes wider and smoother. But this being bog country, you'll get bounced by frost heaves, a ubiquitous feature of northern roads.

From this point the road rolls and climbs slightly back to the summit of the ridge bordering Lake Superior. At 19.8 miles you'll face a decision: Stop and marvel at the stunning lake view or keep rolling down the steep grade. Either way you win, but you should stop to enjoy the vista. Watch for a nasty hump in the surface as you near the bottom.

At 20.5 miles turn left onto Highway 61, and at 21.1 miles turn right onto CR 17. You'll arrive at the monument at 22.1 miles, perhaps ready for a hike along the Grand Portage. After all, the voyageurs didn't have bicycles.

Heartland–Fish Hook Loop

Distance:	24.9 miles
Approximate Pedaling Time:	2 to 3 hours
Terrain:	Mostly flat, with some rolling terrain
Traffic:	Light to moderate on Highway 71, light elsewhere
Surface:	Smooth asphalt
Things to See:	Fish Hook Lake, Dorset, scenic forest and lake area
Facilities:	Restrooms at Heartland Park and Dorset trailheads; restaurants in Park Rapids, Dorset, and Nevis

Park Rapids, which began as a logging camp in 1880, lies in yet another area of transition in Minnesota. If you travel from the western part of the state, you'll notice that the competition between forest and prairie begins to favor the forest. Instead of patches of trees dotting fields of row crops, small clearings of alfalfa and row crops lie amid thick forest. This zone also marks the point where conifers and birch begin edging out oak and maple as the dominant trees.

Besides its location between farmland and forest, Park Rapids also sits about 30 miles south of Itasca State Park, home of Lake Itasca, which forms the headwaters of the Mississippi River. Although the Fish Hook River and assorted lakes surrounding the town don't form the actual headwaters, they do supply the Crow Wing River, an important tributary with a significant history in Minnesota's settlement. Park Rapids also lies near Mantrap Valley, which has several lakes with no apparent outlet. Experts

think that water from this chain of lakes may seep underground before reaching the surface several miles away.

The ride begins in peaceful Heartland Park, which sits on the Fish Hook River. Heartland Park is the type of place where you want to lounge around after a ride. From the park take the trail across the river to East 1st Street, turn right, and follow it about a quarter-mile to North Park Avenue (Highway 71), where you'll turn right again. This street has a wide shoulder and boulevard lined with mature hardwoods, making it a pleasant jaunt out of town.

After riding about 3 miles on Highway 71, turn right onto CR 18. The first 2 miles of this road wind along Fish Hook Lake and through thick stands of pine. The narrow road has a 30-mph speed limit and, after passing the cabins and houses along the shore, reaches a clearing with outstanding views of the lake. Across the lake you can see a fire tower once used by spotters to look for smoke from forest fires.

After leaving the lake, the road widens as it winds and rolls through a mix of pine, hardwoods, pasture and occasional fields of corn and soybeans. At 12.1 miles you'll reach CR 7, which you'll take as part of the short loop. It passes through Dorset, a town of 22 residents that claims to have the most restaurants per capita in the United States. On the first Sunday in August, the town sponsors the Taste of Dorset, a festival of food. Even if you do the long ride, you'll still pass through Dorset, since the Heartland Trail runs through it.

Continuing on the main loop, CR 18 rolls east for another 2 miles, with a graceful curve between two lush swamps marking the final approach to the Heartland Trail at 15.6 miles. Repaved and widened during the summer of 1997, the rail trail features a velvety surface as it winds through a corridor of pine and assorted hardwoods. Unlike trails in southern Minnesota, here you'll see plenty of birch and an occasional lake but no rivers. Yet like its southern cousins, here you'll still see farm fields— this is, after all, Minnesota.

For families with small children, state trails like the Heart-

Ride 24: Heartland–Fish Hook Loop

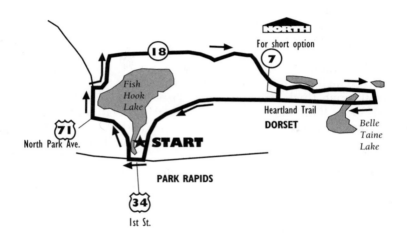

Getting There

From Highway 34 in Park Rapids, turn north on Mill Road and follow it 2 blocks to Heartland Park.

0.0 Take Heartland Trail across the bridge.
0.1 Turn right onto East 1st Street (Highway 34).
0.4 Turn right onto North Park Avenue (Highway 71).
2.9 Turn right onto CR 18.
15.6 Turn right onto Heartland Trail.
24.9 Return to Heartland Park.

Short option:
0.0 Take Heartland Trail across the bridge.
0.1 Turn right onto East 1st Street (Highway 34).
0.4 Turn right onto North Park Avenue (Highway 71).
2.9 Turn right onto CR 18.
12.1 Turn right onto CR 7.
13.1 Turn right onto Heartland Trail.
19.2 Return to Heartland Park.

land offer an excellent alternative to riding on county roads. For a shorter, child-friendly ride, start from Park Rapids and pedal to Dorset, or go from Dorset to Nevis. Of course, ambitious riders can take the trail to Walker, 28 miles from Park Rapids; have lunch on the shore of Leech Lake; and return in time for dinner.

Detroit Lakes Loop

Distance:	18 miles
Approximate Pedaling Time:	1.5 to 2 hours
Terrain:	Mostly flat, with a few rolling hills
Traffic:	Light to moderate
Surface:	Smooth asphalt, with a few rough sections
Things to See:	Detroit Lake, Lakes Sallie and Melissa, rolling glacial landscape
Facilities:	Restrooms and water at park, ice cream and sandwich shop close, all services in Detroit Lakes

If the residents of North Dakota ever decide to try to annex a new resort area, they'll probably lay claim to this land of many lakes. After all, they already have a good start. Detroit Lakes, which sits on a lake of the same name, and many other lakeside towns in this region have become the watery playground for residents of the tabletop-flat Fargo area.

In the 1800s, before our neighbors to the west discovered the lake in large numbers, vacationers arrived by train from St. Paul, Minneapolis, and even Chicago. Upon disembarking, they would board a steamboat for the trip across the lake to one of the resorts that lined the shore. While modes of transportation have changed from train and steamboat to cars, the popularity of this vacation area hasn't altered.

From City Park turn right onto West Lake Drive and enjoy the intimate views of Detroit Lake. You'll ride past the city beach, a narrow strip of sand that on clear days draws sun worshipers in droves. Several years ago a magazine rated this beach one of the best in the nation for swimsuit watching. Although this street can be busy on warm summer days, the 30-mph speed limit and stately trees shading it help it retain a peaceful quality.

At 4.2 miles cross Highway 59, and at 4.4 miles turn right onto CR 22. For the next 2 miles, the rough but ridable road will take you between Lakes Sallie and Melissa. Though cabins crowd the shore, you'll still experience the feeling of northern lake country while cruising through a tunnel of thick foliage. Like many other roads that circle lakes in this area, this one has a low speed limit and generally light traffic.

At 6.3 miles you'll turn right to stay on CR 22, and, after a gentle climb, will emerge from the lowlands surrounding the lake to an undulating landscape of glacial till. Here the road winds among the many small hills, rarely going straight for long as it crosses open fields dotted with ponds and patches of hardwood forest.

At 8.9 miles turn right onto CR 15, which runs north through another area of distinct terrain. For the next 3 miles, this road features much larger rolling hills than anywhere else on the loop. Again you're pedaling up and down courtesy of the glaciers, which were especially active in the region extending from Detroit Lakes to Alexandria. And this being lake country, it seems as if there's a pond at the base of every hill. As you ride along this section, the empty fields, marshes, and quiet countryside offer a refreshing contrast to activity near the more popular lakes.

Turn right onto CR 6 at 12.1 miles. In contrast to the last two pieces of the route, the first mile or so runs straight and mostly level. After passing a gravel pit and entering the outskirts of town, the road becomes smoother and has wide shoulders. You'll ride by a short section of the north shore of Lake Sallie and get a quick view of a quieter part of the lake. Soon after passing the lake, you'll cross Highway 59 again, and 1 mile later you'll turn left onto West Lake Drive, at 16.8 miles. Follow the street back to the park and perhaps enjoy a swim. Or opt for a treat from the nearby ice cream shop—an indulgence that, for some reason, goes perfectly with cycling.

Ride 25: Detroit Lakes Loop

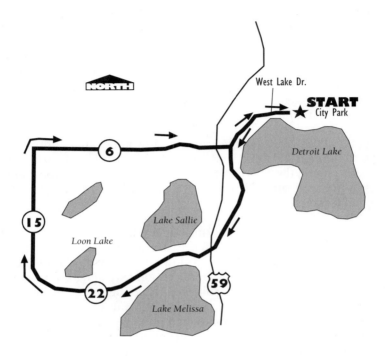

Getting There

From Highway 10 in Detroit Lakes, go south on Washington Avenue about 1 mile, to City Park.

DIREC-TIONS at a glance

0.0 Turn right onto West Lake Drive from the park.

4.2 Cross Highway 59.

4.4 Turn right onto CR 22.

6.3 Turn right to stay on CR 22.

8.9 Turn right onto CR 15.

12.1 Turn right onto CR 6.

15.7 Cross Highway 59.

16.8 Turn left onto West Lake Drive.

18.0 Return to park.

Pelican Lake Loop

Distance:	18.1 miles
Approximate Pedaling Time:	1.5 to 2 hours
Terrain:	Mostly flat, with a few gentle climbs
Traffic:	Light to moderate on CR 9 and CR 35, light elsewhere
Surface:	Smooth asphalt
Things to See:	Pelican Lake, scenic lake country
Facilities:	Resorts along the lake, all services in Pelican Rapids

When you ride this loop, you'll quickly see the intensity of the love affair Minnesotans have with water in general and with lakes in particular. As a popular recreational body of water in this region of countless lakes, Pelican Lake is the perfect example of how residents manifest their feelings for water. Besides buying boats by the thousands, they build cabins. Locals and nonresidents alike build houses of various sizes and shapes close to the shore and close to one another—all so that they can be as close to this object of their affection as possible.

One advantage to cycling in an area with many resorts and cabins is the number and quality of paved roads that you'll find circling and connecting the various lakes. As more people build cabins in these areas, the counties end up paving and widening more roads. Though all these improvements to local roads may ruin the feeling of isolation you may hope for in lake country, it also makes for some incredible riding.

With this in mind, it's no surprise that this loop has excellent roads. They're mostly smooth and quiet, and they wind through forests and fields, while passing the ubiquitous cabins of north woods lake country. Although you won't see anything of historical significance on this route, about halfway between Pelican Rapids and Dunvilla is a historical marker that is well worth visiting.

In 1931 a highway crew found a human skeleton at this site. Archaeologists named the skeleton Minnesota Woman, and estimated it to be 10,000 years old, which makes it one of the oldest found in America. They estimated the woman's age at death to be at 15 and surmised that she drowned in Glacial Lake Pelican, a huge lake that covered the area and adjoined Lake Agassiz, an even larger lake that spanned 80,000 square miles in Minnesota, North Dakota, and three Canadian provinces. It may seem strange, but the clean and clear water in this area eventually drains into the Red River, a muddy stream that flows through one of the flattest places on earth.

After crossing Highway 59, you'll ride for almost 5 miles on South Pelican Lake Road. Although you won't see much of the lake along this road, the extremely smooth surface and the gently rolling landscape of forest and farmland that has just a few short climbs make it a pleasant route that is perfect for a casual ride. At 4.6 miles turn right onto CR 9, which recently received a new coat of blacktop. After about 1 mile the road moves closer to the lake, providing excellent views.

CR 9 changes to CR 20 at about 6 miles and again moves away from the lake. The next 5 miles feature a beautiful surface with wide shoulders. It runs straight over a few gentle rolling hills, and though you won't see the lake, you also won't see cabins jammed next to one another. If you enjoy getting down on the drops and hammering, you'll love this stretch of sweet pavement.

At 11.2 miles turn right onto CR 31, which moves back to the lakeshore. Soon thereafter, at 12.5 miles, you'll turn right onto Fish Lake Road, a quiet lane that closely follows the shoreline. Although cabins line the shore and detract from any pristine lake views you may have hoped for, the route is still pleasant to ride. Most of the cabins and houses seem clean and well maintained and offer another glimpse of life in the heart of lake country.

Ride 26: Pelican Lake Loop

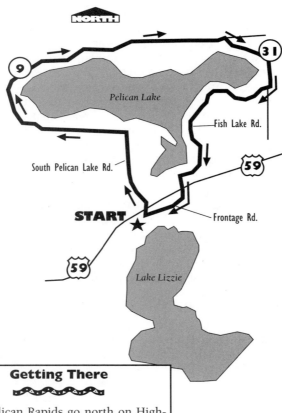

NORTH

9

31

Pelican Lake

Fish Lake Rd.

59

South Pelican Lake Rd.

START

Frontage Rd.

59

Lake Lizzie

Getting There

From Pelican Rapids go north on Highway 59 about 7 miles. Shortly after passing the intersection with Highway 34
west, look for Dunvilla and a hardware
store on the right. Park at either place.

DIREC-TIONS at a glance

0.0	Turn right onto Highway 59 from Dunvilla.
0.1	Turn left onto South Pelican Lake Road (it's actually less than 0.1 mile).
4.6	Turn right onto CR 9.
11.2	Turn right onto CR 31.
12.5	Turn right onto Fish Lake Road.
17.2	Cross Highway 59.
17.3	Turn right onto the frontage road.
18.1	Return to Dunvilla.

At 17.2 miles cross Highway 59 and at 17.3 miles turn right onto the frontage road, which runs close to Lake Lizzie and takes you back to Dunvilla.

Phelps Mill Loop

Distance:	16.3 miles
Approximate Pedaling Time:	1 to 2 hours
Terrain:	Rolling, with one long climb
Traffic:	Light to moderate on CR 1 and CR 35, light elsewhere
Surface:	Mostly smooth asphalt
Things to See:	Phelps Mill (on National Historic Register of Historic Places), scenic lake country
Facilities:	Water and restrooms at park

Don't feel bad if upon parking in the lot at Phelps Mill you decided to skip the ride and spend a couple of hours lounging around this peaceful little settlement. And don't feel like a cycling slacker if you opt to put a canoe in the inviting water of the Otter Tail River, the clear stream that passes through this comfortable park. If this serene National Historic District doesn't make you want to slow down, at least for a moment, you have my sympathy.

Phelps Mill rose along the river during the boom times for milling in Minnesota, when nearly 1,000 such mills operated in the state. It opened in 1889, expanded in 1895, and closed in 1939, a victim of cheaper power and rail transportation.

If you can tear yourself away from the park, a pleasant ride awaits. From the park turn right onto CR 45, a quiet road that for a short distance winds along a marshy area of the Otter Tail. This river starts in the lake and forest country north of here and eventually joins the Bois de Sioux River to form the Red River of the North. A unique characteristic is that Otter Tail flows through so

Ride 27: Phelps Mill Loop

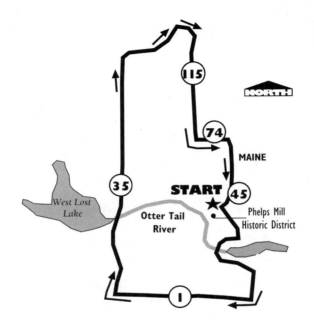

Getting There

From Fergus Falls follow CR 1 east to CR 45 and go north 2.5 miles to Phelps Mill Park.

DIRECTIONS at a glance

0.0 Turn right onto CR 45 from Phelps Mill Park.

1.5 Turn right onto CR 1.

4.0 Turn right onto CR 35.

10.3 Turn right onto CR 115.

12.8 Turn left onto CR 74.

13.8 Go straight onto CR 45.

16.0 Turn right to stay on CR 45.

16.3 Return to park.

many lakes and marshes (50 miles of its 125-mile length is in lakes) that often it's difficult to tell whether it's a river or a long series of connected lakes.

After the short trip on CR 45, turn right onto CR 1 at 1.5 miles. CR 1 will take you almost straight west through an area of small ponds and patches of hardwood forest, with a few gentle curves to make it more interesting. This road carries more traffic than CR 45 but has a wide shoulder, which makes it an excellent cycling route.

At 4.0 miles you'll turn right onto CR 35 and begin a gradual descent to West Lost Lake and the river. After passing the lake, you'll face the longest climb of the ride, a gentle half-mile grade that ascends one of the ridges shaping the countryside. Once you reach the summit, a long, gentle descent takes you to a broad valley floor with huge fields of grasses grown for hay. If you look to your left, you may see the steep glacial moraines that dominate the landscape a few miles to the north near Maplewood State Park.

At 10.3 miles turn right onto CR 115. After a short climb

you're back on the spine of a long, undefined ridge. For more than 2 miles you'll enjoy the smooth surface of this quiet road, which is part of the Otter Tail Scenic Byway. At 12.8 miles turn left onto CR 74, and take the narrow road 1 mile into the town of Maine. The town consists of a church and a funky antiques shop called the Old Maine Store and was the birthplace of Supreme Court Justice William Douglas.

At 13.8 miles go straight to return to CR 45. After a barely noticeable ascent, if you look to the left you'll have an excellent view of a broad forested ridge in the distance. In a perfect cycling world, all rides would end with a descent. And since this ride starts in a nearly perfect rural park, it's appropriate that it should conclude with a downhill.

Near the end of the ride, you'll descend the ridge and cruise around a couple of graceful curves before arriving back in the small settlement of Phelps Mill. At 16.0 miles turn right to stay on CR 45, and 0.3 mile later you're back at the park.

Underwood Loop

Distance:	25.3 miles
Approximate Pedaling Time:	2 to 3 hours
Terrain:	Rolling
Traffic:	Light to moderate on Highway 210, light elsewhere
Surface:	Smooth asphalt
Things to See:	Stalker Lake; rolling mix of forest, farms, and lakes
Facilities:	Convenience stores and restaurants in town close to park

The terrain on this loop includes almost every type of scenery found in Minnesota. You'll pedal past lakes, farm fields, forest, prairie, long ridges, small hills, tall hills, and rolling hills that resemble miniature versions of those covering the Palouse Region of eastern Washington. Besides observing this wide variety of transition landscape, you'll also see ample evidence of Scandinavian immigrants who settled in the region.

If you engage an average Minnesota native in conversation—not always an easy thing to do with these reserved folks—they may eventually claim some Scandinavian heritage. Even if they don't have a drop of Nordic blood in them, it's a safe bet they have relatives or friends who do. And in a state full of solid Scandinavian surnames such as Johnson or Nelson, this region has the serious varieties. Here you'll see names such as Tingvold, Svensvold, Tordenskjold, and others barely pronounceable.

From the neat little town of Underwood, you'll turn left onto Highway 210 for about 2 miles. Although the wide roadbed

eliminates any feeling of intimacy with the landscape, it follows a ridge, and if you look to your right, you'll have good views of the rolling terrain. At 2.5 miles turn right onto CR 119, which takes you away from the highway and deep into the hill and lake country as it gradually descends the ridge.

This mostly smooth road runs almost perfectly straight until a gentle curve provides a view of Stalker Lake. This lake forms the headwaters of the Pomme de Terre River, which in French means "Potato River." Explorers named this Minnesota River tributary after the prairie turnip, a potatolike food of the Sioux. At 8.5 miles turn right onto CR 47 and prepare for some climbing. The next 3 miles mostly ascend, but the climbing comes in large steps, with enough flat stretches to allow for recovery. As is not the case with the short rolling hills common in other parts of the state, the glaciers left more debris in this area, which lies in the Alexandria Moraine.

At 11.4 miles you'll turn right onto CR 12 and face a long, gentle downhill. Of course, what goes down must . . . well, you know the rest, and soon you climb another hill. This stretch of road runs straight for several miles, before some gentle curves deliver you to the peaceful scenery of Johnson Lake. Unlike other lakes in this area, Johnson has few cabins along its marshy shore.

You'll turn right onto CR 39 at 16.5 miles and encounter the most scenic part of the ride. This gorgeous stretch of road winds and rolls between wetlands and forested hills. It also passes the abandoned town of Tordenskjold, which served as the Otter Tail County seat in 1870. The agriculture in this part of Minnesota changes dramatically from that farther south. Instead of huge flat fields, farmers in this region squeeze corn or soybeans into the occasional level spot, while they plant alfalfa and forage grasses on the steep hills.

At 22.8 miles you'll turn right onto CR 35 for a final 2 miles of scenic cycling back to town. This last stretch of road climbs the ridge back to town, winding around smooth, rounded hills.

Although this loop makes a beautiful ride anytime from mid-April through October, try it in early September to enjoy a blend

Ride 28: Underwood Loop

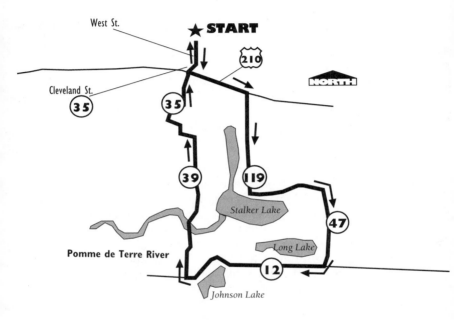

West St.

★ **START**

210

NORTH

Cleveland St.

35

35

39

119

Stalker Lake

47

Pomme de Terre River

Long Lake

12

Johnson Lake

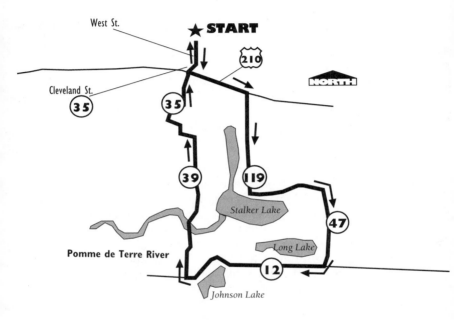

Getting There

From the Twin Cities take I–94 west past St. Cloud and Alexandria to the CR 35/Dalton exit. Turn right and follow CR 35 north to underwood. Follow CR 35 to park.

DIREC-TIONS
at a glance

0.0 Go straight on West Street from Centennial Park.
0.1 Turn right onto Cleveland Street (CR 35).
0.3 Turn left onto Highway 210.
2.5 Turn right onto CR 119.
8.5 Turn right onto CR 47.
11.4 Turn right onto CR 12.
16.5 Turn right onto CR 39.
22.8 Turn right onto CR 35.
25.0 Cross Highway 210.
25.2 Turn left onto West Street.
25.3 Return to Centennial Park.

of nature's finest colors. You'll cycle through a blend of brown wheat stubble, various shades of yellow from maturing soybeans, sparkling blue from lakes and wetlands, and multiple shades of green from the surrounding forest, with a few splashes of red and orange providing a preview of the colorful show yet to come.

Alexandria Loop

Distance:	20.8 miles
Approximate Pedaling Time:	1.5 to 2.5 hours
Terrain:	Rolling hills (longest climb 0.4 mile)
Traffic:	Light to moderate on CR 40 and Highway 27. Light elsewhere.
Surface:	Mostly smooth asphalt, with a couple of moderately rough sections
Things to See:	Scenic forest and farmland, numerous lakes and ponds set among undulating landscape, Runestone Museum (in town, not on ride)
Facilities:	Restrooms; picnic area and water at Lake Brophy Park; many restaurants, motels, and shops in Alexandria

Home to more than 400 lakes, the Alexandria area is one of the most popular vacation destinations for water-crazed Minnesotans. Once a main camping ground for the Ojibwa and Sioux Indians, the region was first explored by fur traders from the Red River area in the 1800s. Both groups undoubtedly would express surprise and shock at what has become of the area. Although still scenic because of the many lakes nestled among rolling hills, the town becomes extremely busy on weekends. Also of note is that PGA golf professional Tom Lehman grew up here.

Besides lakes, Alexandria is home to the Kensington Runestone. Farmer Olaf Ohman found the stone in 1898, and carvings on it depict a journey to this area by Vikings in 1362. From its discovery controversy surrounded the stone, and experts of

Ride 29: Alexandria Loop

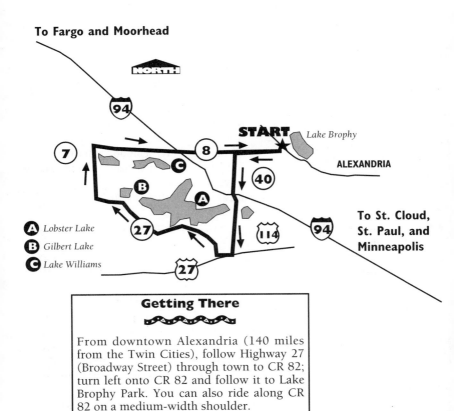

To Fargo and Moorhead

NORTH

94

START · Lake Brophy

7   8

ALEXANDRIA

C

40

B

A

To St. Cloud,
St. Paul, and
Minneapolis

27   114   94

A Lobster Lake
B Gilbert Lake
C Lake Williams

27

Getting There

From downtown Alexandria (140 miles
from the Twin Cities), follow Highway 27
(Broadway Street) through town to CR 82;
turn left onto CR 82 and follow it to Lake
Brophy Park. You can also ride along CR
82 on a medium-width shoulder.

DIREC-TIONS at a glance

0.0 Start at Lake Brophy Park by going straight on CR 8.

1.9 Turn left onto CR 40 (changes to Highway 114 at 3.2 miles).

5.7 Turn right onto Highway 27.

6.4 Turn right onto CR 27.

12.0 Turn right onto CR 7.

14.0 Turn right onto CR 8.

18.9 Cross CR 40.

20.8 Return to park.

the time called it a forgery. In the 1980s more study and discovery of new information on runic inscriptions convinced most that the stone is authentic.

Putting history aside for the moment, this loop begins in Lake Brophy Park, which is a couple of miles west of downtown Alexandria on CR 82. This road is a designated bike route to the park, but it was busy and the pavement was only fair. From the park cross CR 82 and follow CR 8. At 1.9 miles turn left onto CR 40, which changes to Highway 114 at 3.2 miles. This section of the ride is the least interesting, as it descends and crosses under I–94. Before dropping down the long hill, you'll have a good view of the surrounding countryside. Immediately after crossing the interstate, you'll pass Lobster Lake. Named after the crustacean for its shape and not its contents, the lake contains muskies, an aggressive member of the pike family.

At 5.7 miles turn right onto Highway 27, a moderately busy state highway. It has a small shoulder, and you'll ride on the highway for a short distance. At 6.4 miles turn right onto CR 27 and get ready for some awesome cycling. This smooth black ribbon climbs over numerous small hills and winds around sparkling ponds tucked into small hollows of hardwood forest. If the lack of traffic and the glorious pavement don't bring a huge smile to your face, the soothing scenery should do the job.

At 12.0 miles you'll emerge from the woods to turn right onto CR 7. Although you'll be out of the thick forest on this straight stretch of road, the open fields and rolling hills will combine to provide scenic views of the area.

At 14.0 miles turn right onto CR 8. Expansion cracks—courtesy of the freeze-thaw cycle—make this section a bit rough, but it's still decent pavement. After crossing back over the interstate and conquering the longest climb, you'll reenter a short section of forest. Though not as scenic as the CR 27 section, it's a welcome change from open fields. At 18.9 miles you'll reach CR 40 again; stay on CR 8 and follow it straight back to the park.

Option

For a longer ride that for several years was the actual course for the state road-race championships, do not turn at Highway 27. Continue south on Highway 114 for 5.2 miles to CR 26 and turn right. This fun road has lots of curves and rolling hills, and it passes many ponds and wetlands. At 13.9 miles turn right onto CR 7 and follow the directions for the shorter loop. This optional loop totals 29.7 miles.

Lake Osakis Loop

Distance:	19.1 miles
Approximate Pedaling Time:	1.5 to 3 hours
Terrain:	Mostly flat, with a couple of short, gentle rolling hills
Traffic:	Moderate on Highway 27 and CR 3. Light elsewhere.
Surface:	Mostly smooth asphalt, with a couple of moderately rough sections
Things to See:	Lake Osakis, scenic forest and farm-land, resort town of Osakis
Facilities:	Restrooms, picnic area, and playground at town park; a couple of restaurants in town; gift shops and small store at Linwood Resort along the lake

Lake country begins in the northern third of Minnesota. Although the southern and central parts of the state have their share, the North has a monopoly on the number of lakes. Besides being a popular destination, Lake Osakis is called the Mother Walleye Lake. Each year the state catches and harvests eggs from walleye (the Minnesota state fish) and uses them to stock thirty other lakes. After harvesting, the state returns the fish to the lake, hence the name.

This loop begins at the Osakis town park on the shore of Lake Osakis. After a short jaunt through town, you'll turn onto CR 3 and ride it back to the lakeshore. This stretch has the roughest pavement and the most traffic, but it's short at just over a mile and not as busy as the norm for most urbanites.

The next stretch of road, on CR 10, brings you back closer to the lake. The first 2.8 miles are narrow and don't have a shoulder but shouldn't have much traffic most of the time. Try to avoid this section on Friday nights and Sunday afternoons, when people are arriving and departing from their cabins. I recommend riding this loop early on Saturday or Sunday or almost anytime on weekdays.

At about 5 miles into the ride, the pavement improves dramatically, with the road becoming wider and much smoother. The road along this side of the lake is mostly flat and offers good views of the lake. At 10.9 miles you'll turn right onto CR 37, which winds away from the lake. This part of the ride features 5 miles of beautiful pavement, light traffic, rolling hills, and occasional views of the lake from a higher vantage point than at any other section of the loop. The road also winds through a few small farms carved out of the hardwood forest.

After a fun gradual descent, turn right onto Highway 27 for 0.1 mile, and take a quick right onto CR 55. The next 2 miles offer a dramatic contrast to the preceding 5. This narrow, lightly traveled road snakes along the lakeshore, which at times is just feet away. If you want intimate views of the lake, you'll love this soothing section of the loop. Huge trees form a canopy along the lake and provide welcome shade after you've ridden through fields. Linwood Resort has a small store and offers a good place to stop for a break.

At 18.6 miles turn right at the stop sign, which is Lake Street. Follow this quiet residential street back to the park.

Family option

Most of this loop isn't suitable for children, unless they're riding a tandem with an adult. For a more child-friendly ride, or for anyone who wants a short ride, reverse the directions and ride along CR 55 immediately upon turning off Lake Street. Follow CR 55 to where it ends at Highway 27 and return the same way. This 5.6-mile out-and-back ride would provide a casual, relaxing ride along the scenic lakeshore.

145

Ride 30: Lake Osakis Loop

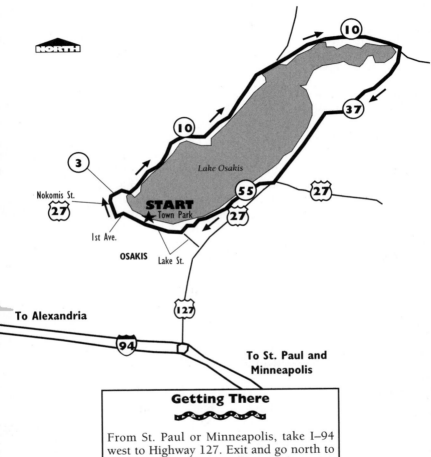

Getting There

From St. Paul or Minneapolis, take I–94 west to Highway 127. Exit and go north to the T stop sign. Go straight to Highway 27, under the bridge, and take the first left, which is 8th Avenue East. Follow 8th Avenue East to the stop sign on Lake Street, turn left, and go 1 block to the city park, which is on the right side of the street.

DIREC-TIONS at a glance

0.0 Start at the town park in Osakis by turning right onto Lake Street.
0.5 Turn left onto 1st Avenue.
0.7 Turn right onto Nokomis Street (Highway 27).
1.1 Turn right onto CR 3.
2.3 Turn right onto CR 10.
5.1 Pavement improves!
10.9 Turn right onto CR 37.
16.2 Turn right onto Highway 27.
16.3 Turn right onto CR 55.
18.0 Stay to the right.
18.6 Turn right at stop sign (Lake Street).
19.1 Return to town park.

Family option:
0.0 Turn left onto Lake Street from park.
0.5 Turn left onto CR 55.
2.8 CR 55 ends at Highway 27.
Return to town.

Albany Loop

Distance:	19.1 miles
Approximate Pedaling Time:	1.5 to 2.5 hours
Terrain:	Rolling hills, with a 1-mile climb
Traffic:	Light
Surface:	Smooth asphalt
Things to See:	Lakes, ponds, wetlands, beautiful rolling hills; mix of forest, farms, and pasture
Facilities:	Convenience store and small grocery store in town; motels, restaurants, and other services in St. Cloud (20 miles south)

Compared with other rides in this book, this one won't take you past any sights of major historical significance or through any incredibly scenic parks or gorgeous river valleys. But what it lacks in these attributes it makes up for in versatility. Casual riders can take the short loop and miss a mile-long climb while saving almost 5 miles. The more hard-core can do the full loop and get a decent workout on the ascent.

This ride is also an excellent option for those who need to get out for a quick leg-stretching ride after sitting in a vehicle all day while traveling to an area destination. It's also perfect for Twin Cities residents looking for an alternative to their usual weekday rides from home.

Like the Avon Loop and the St. Joseph Loop, this one rolls through the beautiful countryside of Stearns County. Though the scenery doesn't have the stunning qualities of southeastern Minnesota or the North Shore of Lake Superior, it does have the

Ride 31: Albany Loop

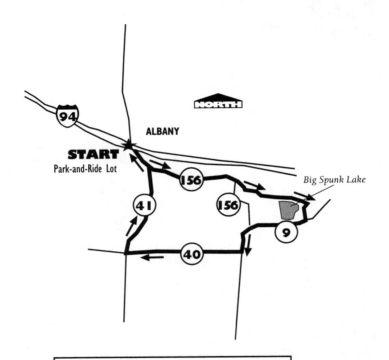

Getting There

From the Twin Cities take I–94 west past St. Cloud to Albany (exit 147). Turn left, cross the freeway, turn right onto CR 41, and depart from the park-and-ride lot.

DIREC-TIONS at a glance

0.0	Turn left from lot onto CR 41.
0.7	Turn left onto CR 156.
7.6	Turn right onto CR 9.
11.0	Turn right onto CR 40.
15.1	Turn right onto CR 41.
19.1	Return to park-and-ride lot.

Short option:

0.0	Turn left from lot on CR 41.
0.7	Turn left on CR 156.
5.1	Turn right to stay on CR 156.
6.1	Turn right onto CR 9.
7.1	Turn right onto CR 40.
11.2	Turn right onto CR 41.
15.2	Return to park-and-ride lot.

right mix of marshes, lakes, forests, and farm fields to provide a soothing country jaunt.

The loop begins in the park-and-ride lot just off the freeway. After a quick spin on CR 41, turn left onto CR 156, which features almost ideal pavement. This road parallels the freeway for about 2.5 miles before it breaks the link and turns south. This section is the epitome of a perfect cycling road: It's smooth, it's quiet, and after running straight at first it has several swooping turns that pull your bike into them with only a slight lean from the rider. All you need to do is sit back and enjoy the ride. And pedal, too.

At 5.1 miles the casual or late-for-a-function-but-had-to-get-a-ride-in can turn right to stay on CR 156. This mile-long segment has more of the same ultrasmooth blacktop and will put you several miles ahead of the partner who wants to do the long version. And, of course, whoever takes this shortcut becomes a rabbit for the others to chase.

For those doing the long loop, continue straight on the main road as it winds through a neighborhood on Big Spunk Lake. At 7.6 miles turn right onto CR 9. You'll face a quick warm-up climb, followed by the mile-long one a short distance later. If climbing isn't your favorite part of cycling, remember that what goes up must come down. Moreover, after reaching the crest you'll have a curvy half-mile-long downhill.

After enjoying a few curves on CR 9, at 11 miles turn right onto CR 40. The half-mile long climb shouldn't be a problem, since you've already done the big one. Those who took the cut-off may be sweating it out some, but it's a gradual grade. CR 40 runs almost yardstick straight through scenic rolling farmland and provides good views to the south of a thick carpet of trees covering distant hills.

At 15.1 miles turn right onto CR 41. This road carries more traffic than the others, but it's still relatively quiet. From here it's a mostly straight shot back to Albany. If you're part of a group that split up at the 5-mile mark, this may be the place where you catch up or get caught. But if you're part of the long-loop group and haven't caught the others, this last 4-mile section could get interesting. Hammer away and have fun. Loser buys the ice cream.

Avon Loop

Distance:	22.7 miles
Approximate Pedaling Time:	1.5 to 3 hours
Terrain:	Rolling hills, with numerous short climbs and one 0.5-mile climb
Traffic:	Light
Surface:	Smooth asphalt
Things to See:	Lakes, ponds, wetlands, beautiful rolling hills; mix of forest, farms, and pasture
Facilities:	Convenience store and small grocery store in town; outhouse at boat landing on Middle Spunk Lake, numerous motels, restaurants, and other services in St. Cloud (15 miles south)

As one of the largest outstate towns in Minnesota, St. Cloud sits on the Mississippi amid scenic countryside 75 miles from the Twin Cities. The town founder named St. Cloud after the hometown of Napoléon Bonaparte. The surrounding area contains large deposits of granite and many quarries, which gave St. Cloud the nickname of Granite City. With three colleges contributing to St. Cloud's culture, as well as plenty of motels and restaurants, the city makes an excellent base for exploring the roads of Stearns County.

This loop begins at Avon, about 15 miles northwest of St. Cloud. While cruising along the quiet county roads of this ride, I couldn't help thinking that I had stumbled onto the best-kept cycling secret in Minnesota. There appeared to be no end to the number of loops a cyclist could explore, thanks in part to more

paved roads than in many other parts of rural Minnesota. As in Wisconsin, more country roads were paved in dairy country so that milk trucks could reach farms in all kinds of weather. And this is dairy country.

From the Avon Middle School, follow CR 9 south through town. After crossing the interstate and turning left onto CR 50, you'll pass through the ugliest portion of this loop. Sandwiched between I–94 on the left and several businesses on the right, you may wonder what's so great about this route. Be patient. After just over a half-mile, you'll turn right to stay on CR 50 and trade the noise of the freeway for the serenity of the rural countryside.

For the next 7.8 miles, this sweet road with a good shoulder takes riders through some of the most scenic landscape in central Minnesota. But be prepared to climb, since this road features numerous rolling hills. Although none ascends for more than a few tenths of a mile, the first 5 miles have plenty of them. Take your time, relax, and enjoy the soothing blend of hardwood forest, ponds, and farms.

At about 9.4 miles turn right onto 260th Street and get ready to savor more than 3 miles of incredible riding. The first 2 miles of this road run straight before turning ninety degrees right, followed by a 90-degree left 0.3 mile later. The final stretch, which becomes Manana Road, features more smooth pavement and sinuous curves. This section of the loop is also the flattest and represents the epitome of a quiet country lane.

At 12.8 miles turn right onto CR 9. On the right you'll pass a wildlife refuge, while on the left is a ridge that you don't have to worry about climbing. At about 18.3 miles the pavement becomes smoother, with the added feature of a good shoulder. This also marks the beginning of the longest climb, a steady grade of a half-mile. Although you may not like this aspect of the route, you'll love the next one. After reaching the crest, a nearly 1-mile descent awaits riders. The descent drops steeply for a while before it changes to a swooping, gradual downhill that will draw your bike through the gentle curves.

Of course, the variation of the old adage of what goes up

Ride 32: Avon Loop

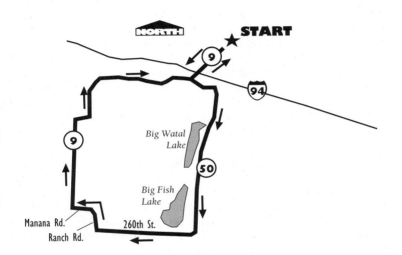

NORTH

START

Big Watal Lake

Big Fish Lake

Manana Rd.

Ranch Rd.

260th St.

Getting There

From the Twin Cities take I–94 west past St. Cloud (about 70 miles northwest) to Avon (exit 153). Turn right and follow CR 9 for 0.8 mile to the Avon Middle School. Depart from here.

DIRECTIONS at a glance

0.0 Turn left from the school onto CR 9.
0.9 Cross I–94 and turn left onto CR 50.
1.6 Turn right to stay on CR 50.
9.4 Turn right onto 260th Street.
11.8 Stay right onto Ranch Road.
12.1 Left onto Manana Road.
12.8 Right onto CR 9.
22.7 Return to school.

must come down applies with a short but gradual climb after this luscious descent. Unfortunately, the loop ends too soon as you return to the bridge over the interstate and the short trip through town back to the school. If people stare at you as you pass through town, it's probably because of the wide smile on your face after an awesome ride.

Dairy Country Tour

Distance:	18 or 20 miles
Approximate Pedaling Time:	1.5 to 2.5 hours
Terrain:	Rolling hills, with several short climbs and one 0.3-mile climb
Traffic:	Moderate on CR 2. Light elsewhere.
Surface:	Smooth asphalt
Things to See:	Lakes, ponds, wetlands, beautiful rolling hills; mix of forest, farms, and pasture
Facilities:	Nothing at the park-and-ride lot; convenience stores and the Meeting Grounds coffee shop (perfect place for postride refreshments) in St. Joseph; numerous motels, restaurants, and other services in St. Cloud (4 miles east)

As you drive west on I–94 from the Twin Cities to St. Cloud, the unremarkable scenery rolls by for part of the journey. The mostly flat landscape features a few interstate exits complete with the ubiquitous truck stops, fast-food joints, and little else. But as you close in on St. Cloud, you'll notice the terrain changing dramatically.

Instead of nondescript fields and strip malls, the landscape has become a rolling green carpet of large hills, broad valleys, and thick forests. Thoughtfully carved out by active glaciers, the suddenly scenic terrain lies west of St. Cloud. Dairy farms and ponds dot the area, and many miles of smooth, quiet roads wind throughout the county. It may not be cycling nirvana, but it's close.

Ride 33: Dairy Country Tour

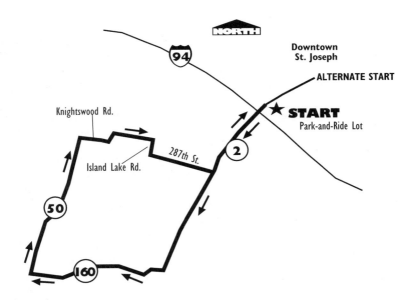

Getting There

From the Twin Cities take I–94 west past St. Cloud (about 70 miles northwest) to St. Joseph (exit 160). Turn right and park in the park-and-ride lot. To start from town, follow CR 2 1 mile to downtown St. Joseph.

**DIREC-
TIONS
at a glance**

0.0 Turn left from the park-and-ride lot onto
   CR 2.
2.6 Turn right onto CR 160.
8.0 Turn right onto CR 50.
11.2 Turn right onto Knightswood Road.
13.6 Turn right onto Island Lake Road.
14.1 Turn left onto 287th Street.
16.5 Turn left onto CR 2.
18.0 Return to park-and-ride lot.

This ride begins in either St. Joseph, a small town with the largest community of Benedictine women in the world, or a park-and-ride lot 1 mile west of town at the intersection of CR 2 and I–94. The Meeting Grounds, a cool little coffee shop downtown, is the perfect place from which to begin the ride. If you decide to ride from here the total distance of this loop increases to 20 miles.

From the park-and-ride lot, turn left and go west on CR 2, a flat road that is moderately busy but has a wide, smooth shoulder. At 2.6 miles you'll turn right onto CR 160 and confront a short climb to the top of a ridge. If you don't like climbing, try to remember that you'll ride back down it on a different road later in the loop.

After cresting the ridge, the road winds through the rolling landscape. This section of the route lets the rider get into a rhythm that only gently rolling terrain allows. None of the small hills on most of CR 160 require the rider to stand to power over them. Instead, the gentle undulations provide just the correct amount of momentum on the descents to assist in a smooth ascent. The scenery along this road ranges from forest, to row crops, to fields of fragrant alfalfa. Besides these visual treats, the sweet and sour aromas of the country surround you, especially after a farmer has cut a field of brilliant green grass or clover.

At 8.0 miles turn right onto CR 50, which is part of the Avon Loop. Though you may have ridden this road as part of the other loop, this ride takes you in the opposite direction. At 11.2 miles turn right onto Knightswood Road. For the next 5 miles, you'll ride smooth, quiet country lanes instead of major county roads. On these narrow blacktop ribbons you'll experience an intimacy with the land that you can't feel on wider roads. Trees and bushes crowd closer to the road, providing a green curtain that seems to take cyclists one step further from the hectic pace of everyday life.

As I reviewed my notes, I noticed the word *gorgeous* written twice to describe this part of the ride. Since writers often tend to use too many superlatives in describing things, I'll let the above adjective serve as the description of this section of the loop. All I can add is that the hills are short rollers and that you'll see virtually no traffic. At 13.6 miles turn right onto Island Lake Road, and at 14.1 miles turn left onto 287th Street. Before reaching CR 2, you'll get to descend the ridge you climbed a few miles back.

At 16.5 miles turn left onto CR 2 for the short spin back to the park-and-ride lot or the town. If you're like my friend Henry and me, you'll stop back at the coffee shop to savor the ride as well as the postride refreshments.

Lake Minnewaska Loop

Distance:	20.3 miles
Approximate Pedaling Time:	1.5 to 3 hours
Terrain:	Mostly flat, with rolling hills
Traffic:	Moderate on Highway 29 and 28. Light elsewhere.
Surface:	Mostly decent asphalt, with a 6-mile stretch of rough pavement
Things to See:	Lake Minnewaska, glacial ridge surrounding lake, Indian burial mounds, Glacial Lakes State Park, Pope County Museum across from city beach
Facilities:	Restrooms at beach start; stores and restaurants in town, which is close to beach; Dairy Queen at halfway point, in Starbuck

As you drive into Glenwood from the north or the east, a startling view of Lake Minnewaska unfolds about 1 mile from town. After you've cruised along on flat to barely rolling highways, the road suddenly drops down a glacial ridge that surrounds Glenwood and its watery neighbor. The lake appears almost as if it's a mythical apparition, brought on by the shock of finding the large body of water in the middle of farm country.

Thanks to Lake Minnewaska—the thirteenth largest lake in Minnesota—Glenwood has developed into a resort town as well as a supply point for area farmers. The town lies in a part of the state that retains dramatic evidence of glacial activity. From the steep ridge along the north and east side of Minnewaska to the long, gradual steps that ascend for 2 miles and the relentless

rolling hills of the south shore, the landscape has obviously been sculpted by glaciers. Glacial Lakes State Park, located south of Starbuck, lies in rugged terrain scoured by glaciers. The north shore of the lake has several Indian burial mounds, but they're difficult to spot because they blend into the rolling countryside.

From the beach the route follows appropriately named South Lake Shore Drive along the south shore. Although it's a narrow road, the 30-mph speed limit makes the ride safe and relaxing. Mature oaks and assorted hardwoods form an endless wall of green to your left, while the lake extends nearly 2 miles across the valley to your right. After a couple of miles, the road widens in an area of new housing, before narrowing and then ending at CR 18.

Turn right at 5.2 miles on CR 18. The road has the requisite expansion cracks that can cause a slightly bumpy ride, but great views of the lake make up for any minor jolts. Since the roads have climbed some from the shore, you'll now have scenic vistas of Minnewaska contrasted against the imposing ridge that rises across the lake. This road has plenty of short rolling hills to keep the ride interesting and perhaps your heart rate up a couple of beats if you wish.

At 9.7 miles turn right onto the bike path that parallels Highway 29. This is a busy highway, with no shoulder and poor pavement, so avoid the highway. The path has a couple of short breaks upon entering Starbuck and ends at 11.4 miles. By now you're only a couple of blocks from the next turn, and the road widens through town. With the state park just south of town, maybe the state will improve Highway 29 by adding shoulders or running a paved path to the park.

Turn right onto Highway 28 at 11.6 miles. Fortunately, this road has a shoulder, since it carries plenty of traffic, but the pavement is rough. Since this is a major highway in only fair shape, perhaps the state will repave it soon. But you're on it for just over 5 miles before entering Long Beach, a sort of suburb of Glenwood. At 17.2 miles turn right onto CR 54 to leave the highway and return to the lake, and at 19.5 miles stay right on

Ride 34: Lake Minnewaska Loop

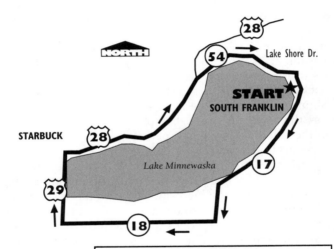

Getting There

From St. Paul or Minneapolis (about 100 miles), take Highway 55 west to Glenwood, turn left on South Franklin (Highway 104), and go about 0.6 mile to the city beach.

DIREC-TIONS at a glance

0.0	Turn right from beach onto South Lake Shore Drive (CR 17).
5.2	Turn right onto CR 18.
9.7	Turn right onto Highway 29 (take the paved bike path along the highway).
11.6	Turn right onto Highway 28.
17.2	Turn right onto CR 54.
19.5	Stay right on Lake Shore Drive.
20.0	Right onto South Franklin.
20.3	Return to beach.

Lake Shore Drive. To finish, turn right onto South Franklin at 20.0 miles and follow it to the beach, at 20.3 miles. After you finish the ride, you may want to visit the Pope County Museum which is across South Lake Shore Drive from the beach. For a modest fee you can look at displays of Helbing Indian artifacts and see replicas of a blacksmith's shop, trapper's cabin, and Indian camp.

Options

Much of this ride isn't suitable for children. As with the Lake Osakis Loop, though, an easy out-and-back ride exists. Families or casual cyclists looking for an easy ride can cruise out-and-back on South Lake Shore Drive (CR 17) to the intersection with CR 18 for a 10.4-mile trip. For an even shorter out-and-back ride (about 6 miles), turn left from the beach and do the last 3 miles of the long loop. Both of these shorter rides follow quiet, mostly residential streets and provide excellent views of the lake.

Lake Traverse and Prairie Pothole Tour

Distance:	27.5 miles
Approximate Pedaling Time:	2 to 3.5 hours
Terrain:	Mostly flat, with some long, gentle climbs along the lake
Traffic:	Mostly light
Surface:	Smooth asphalt
Things to See:	Traverse County Park, Lake Traverse, scores of wetlands dotting scenic farm fields, views of South Dakota ridge along the lake
Facilities:	Restrooms and water at park; small grocery, cafe, and art gallery in Browns Valley

To peruse a map of Minnesota, it's easy to overlook this part of the state, even though it bulges noticeably along an otherwise straight border with South Dakota. Many residents probably don't realize that Browns Valley straddles the major drainage ridge that separates water flowing north to Hudson Bay from water flowing south and east to the Mississippi.

The town also sits between two important bodies of water. As the source of the Bois de Souix River, Lake Traverse to the north is a major part of the headwaters of the Red River, which flows north to Hudson Bay. Big Stone Lake to the south forms the headwaters of the Minnesota River, which merges with the Mississippi in the Twin Cities.

Before you begin riding, when you're still 20 miles east of Browns Valley you'll notice a ridge on the western horizon. The

Ride 35: Lake Traverse and Prairie Pothole Tour

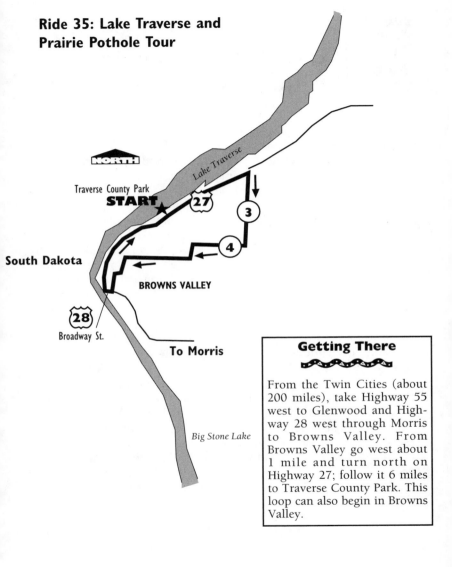

NORTH

Lake Traverse

Traverse County Park
START

27

3

4

South Dakota

BROWNS VALLEY

28

Broadway St.

To Morris

Big Stone Lake

Getting There

From the Twin Cities (about 200 miles), take Highway 55 west to Glenwood and Highway 28 west through Morris to Browns Valley. From Browns Valley go west about 1 mile and turn north on Highway 27; follow it 6 miles to Traverse County Park. This loop can also begin in Browns Valley.

DIREC-TIONS
at a glance

0.0 Leave Traverse County Park and turn left onto Highway 27.

5.9 Turn right onto CR 3.

10.5 Turn right onto CR 4.

20.9 Turn right onto Broadway Street (Highway 28) in Browns Valley.

21.5 Turn right onto Highway 27.

27.5 Arrive back at park.

ridge is the South Dakota border, and it forms a striking contrast to the flat fields that dominate this part of western Minnesota. Besides being a major farming area, the two lakes and surrounding countryside provide an exceptional habitat for a wide variety of waterfowl, including pelicans.

The first section of this loop follows Highway 27 along the east shore of Lake Traverse. Although it's a state highway, the smooth pavement, narrow but decent shoulders, and light traffic make this a good cycling road. It climbs gradually along the ridge and winds through thick forests of oak and cottonwood, while still offering excellent views of the lake. If you're lucky, you may see wild turkeys along this road.

At 5.9 miles turn right onto CR 3 and climb a short hill to the top of the ridge. The landscape changes suddenly and dramatically, from forests and small clearings to huge fields of wheat, corn, and soybeans. This road climbs gradually along the ridge, and it features scenic views of the western shore of Lake Traverse.

At 10.5 miles turn right onto CR 4, a poorly marked intersection. As with the previous road, you'll also have some excellent

171

views of the lake. One unique aspect of this area is the large number of small wetlands—called potholes—that dot the fields. Formed by glaciers, these small ponds and swamps provide valuable habitat for waterfowl, especially for breeding.

Unfortunately, farmers drained many of these miniature ecosystems during the 1970s as they responded to high commodity prices by planting every available acre. The good news is that many farmers have restored potholes within the past few years. Unlike the huge uniform fields common in other parts of the state, these small swamps seem to lessen the impact of human beings on the landscape by breaking up long straight rows of crops.

At 20 miles you'll drop abruptly into Browns Valley and will pass a junkyard, the only ugly feature of this ride. Fortunately, you're going downhill at this point and can zip past it. Turn right onto Broadway Street (Highway 28) and follow it as it curves to the right out of town. At 21.5 miles turn right onto Highway 27 and follow it 6 miles back to the park.

Option

To get most of the climbing done early, you can start the loop in town. You'll get the long gradual ascents on Highway 27 out of the way early in the ride. Another option is to ride this loop reversed, heading toward town first. You'll have one long climb out of Browns Valley (0.6 mile), but much of the route will descend gradually. Unfortunately, this isn't a route for children, unless they're riding a tandem with an adult.

Lake That Speaks Loop

Distance:	18.7 miles
Approximate Pedaling Time:	1.5 to 3 hours
Terrain:	Mostly flat, with a couple of short, gentle rolling hills
Traffic:	Light
Surface:	Smooth asphalt
Things to See:	Lac Qui Parle State Park and Wildlife Refuge, Lac Qui Parle Lake scenic farmland
Facilities:	Restrooms, small bait store across from parking lot for water (should bring own water and food)

If by some strange occurrence this ride were suddenly 30 miles from the Twin Cities, it would quickly become a favorite of many riders. But since it's located in essentially the middle of nowhere, it's highly doubtful you'll encounter other riders on this loop. What you will see, however, is a lake that is one of the most prolific breeding grounds in Minnesota for geese and other waterfowl.

Lac Qui Parle means "Lake That Speaks," and this wide spot in the Minnesota River does that during waterfowl migration, when hundreds of thousands of ducks, geese, swans, and pelicans pass through the area. Besides the state park, a 32,000-acre wildlife refuge surrounds the lake, providing habitat for 229 species of birds. Part of the beauty of this ride is the isolation and feeling of stepping back to a time before asphalt and assorted two- and four-wheel machines.

After leaving the parking lot, you'll ride along the western shore of the lake for just over 8 miles. A short, gradual climb

brings you to the top of a ridge that provides scenic views of the lake. Since Lac Qui Parle lies in a prairie, you won't find thick forest obscuring views of it. Stands of dead trees remain as a stark reminder that this is a river with water levels that fluctuate dramatically compared with those of normal lakes.

After you've ridden a few miles on the ridge, the road drops back to lake level and changes to CR 33. You're still on the correct road, so just keep pedaling and enjoy the scenery. At about 8.3 miles, turn right onto Highway 40 and cross the lake before turning right onto CR 31. This latter smooth road will take you away from the lake as it climbs a ridge on the east shore and winds past neat farms and through fields of corn, soybeans, and wheat. Minnesota doesn't produce as much wheat as states farther south and west, and farmers in the drier western counties plant most of it. The road ascends the east ridge gently and provides beautiful views of the sparkling lake when it curves back to the west.

Since many lakes in Minnesota have become crowded with cabins, it's refreshing to see Lac Qui Parle sitting grandly in its natural state among the prairie grasses. To some it may look scruffy, with dead trees and low bushes crowding the shore, while huge cottonwoods dominate the rest of the landscape. But this is perhaps the most unspoiled and wild lake you'll find without traveling to extreme northeastern Minnesota.

At 14.5 miles you'll take a right onto Highway 7, and at 14.7 miles another right onto CR 32. You're probably getting tired of hearing about climbing ridges, but there's one more short, easy one to go over. At the crest of the hill is a scenic overlook perched high above the lake. While it's tempting to blast down the hill, it's well worth stopping to take in the spectacular view. About halfway down the hill, an observation deck juts off the roadway and provides yet another beautiful vista of Lac Qui Parle.

If you stopped, enjoy the rest of the descent. If because of an adrenaline rush from the downhill you didn't stop, you missed some incredible views of the lake. At the bottom of the hill, you'll arrive at CR 13 and the parking area. Of course, if you missed the scenic overlooks you can always ride back up to them.

Ride 36: Lake That Speaks Loop

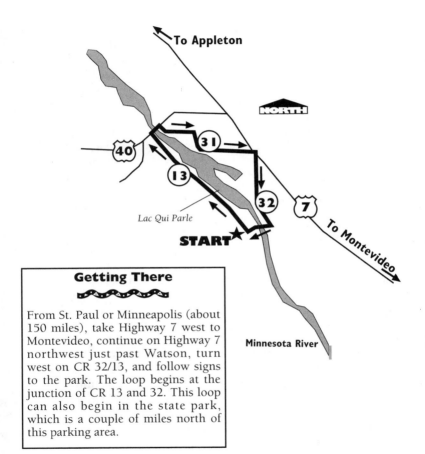

To Appleton

NORTH

40

31

13

Lac Qui Parle

32

7

To Montevideo

START

Minnesota River

Getting There

From St. Paul or Minneapolis (about 150 miles), take Highway 7 west to Montevideo, continue on Highway 7 northwest just past Watson, turn west on CR 32/13, and follow signs to the park. The loop begins at the junction of CR 13 and 32. This loop can also begin in the state park, which is a couple of miles north of this parking area.

DIREC-TIONS at a glance

0.0	Leave lot and turn left onto CR 13.
8.3	Turn right onto Highway 40.
9.0	Turn right onto CR 31.
14.5	Turn right onto Highway 7.
14.7	Turn right onto CR 32.
17.5	Scenic overlook on right side of road.
17.8	Observation deck overlooking lake.
18.7	Return to parking area.

Montevideo Loop

Distance:	12.7 miles
Approximate Pedaling Time:	1 to 1.5 hours
Terrain:	Mostly flat, with a couple of short, gentle rolling hills
Traffic:	Light
Surface:	Smooth asphalt
Things to See:	Minnesota River Valley, neat farms, scenic farmland
Facilities:	Convenience store at trailhead; restaurants, shops, and motels in Montevideo

Named for the capital of Uruguay, Montevideo lies at the confluence of the Chippewa and Minnesota Rivers in western Minnesota. The Minnesota town maintains a sister-city relationship with its South American namesake and even has a bronze statue of José Artigas, a hero of Uruguayan independence, in the downtown mall.

The steep wooded valleys and bluffs make this an interesting oasis amid thousands of acres of farm fields. Besides the usual crops of corn and soybeans, observant riders may notice a leafy plant that resembles a romaine type of lettuce. The plant you're seeing is the sugar beet, and Minnesota is the number one producer in the nation. Although the Red River Valley produces most of the sugar beets in the state, farmers from Montevideo east toward Willmar grow and process a significant amount of this crop.

Montevideo is just 10 miles south of Lac Qui Parle State Park, site of the Lac Qui Parle Mission, the first Protestant mis-

Ride 37: Montevideo Loop

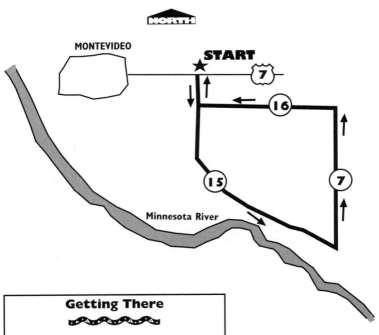

Getting There

From St. Paul or Minneapolis (about 150 miles), take Highway 7 west to Montevideo. On the north end of town, look for CR 15 and a convenience store with a huge parking lot. The bike path starts across from this store.

DIRECTIONS at a glance

0.0 Leave lot and turn left onto bike path that parallels CR 15.
4.8 Bike path ends; ride on road.
5.7 Turn left onto CR 7.
7.9 Turn left onto CR 16.
10.6 Turn right onto CR 15 and bike path.
12.7 Return to parking lot.

sion in Minnesota. Residents of the mission, which was established in 1835, wove cloth for the first time in the state, and translated the Bible into the Dakota language, for which they devised a written alphabet. Lac Qui Parle also provides a refuge for a large population of waterfowl, especially during spring and autumn.

This short loop begins at a convenience store on the east edge of town. A new paved path parallels the road for nearly 5 miles. The path passes several housing developments on the way to Wegdahl, a group of grain elevators located on the Minnesota River. The path ends here, but follow the lightly traveled road up and away from the river.

At 5.7 miles turn left onto CR 7, the epitome of a country road that goes mostly straight through brilliant green fields. At 7.9 miles turn left onto CR 16 and follow it for about 2.5 miles, back to CR 15. Cross CR 15 to the bike path, turn right, and 2 miles later you're back at your vehicle.

Although this loop isn't all that unique and doesn't offer spectacular scenery, it's a pleasant jaunt for cyclists who don't want to ride far but do want a taste of quiet rural riding. Families can stay on the path to the end, turn around, and return to the start for an easy 10-mile out-and-back trip, or ride a couple of miles out-and-back for even a shorter trip.

Options

Riders who want more mileage can easily add 7 or 8 miles to this loop by turning right onto CR 15 instead of left onto CR 7 at the 5.7-mile mark. At CR 6 turn left and follow it up to CR 16, where you'll take another left. Stay on CR 16, which will take you back to CR 15 and the bike path. This loop follows smooth and virtually traffic-free roads.

Norway and Games Lake Loop

Distance:	19.0 miles
Approximate Pedaling Time:	1.5 to 2.5 hours
Terrain:	Flat to rolling
Traffic:	Moderate on Highway 9, light elsewhere
Surface:	Mostly smooth asphalt
Things to See:	Glacial lakes area, scenic lakes, farmland
Facilities:	Water, restrooms, beach, and snacks at county park

Sometimes you find the best rides in unlikely places. It's similar to walking into a dumpy-looking little restaurant and having the best meal of your life. The landscape around Game and Norway Lakes seems to fall within yet another transition zone. To the south the land flattens into superb yet featureless farmland, while to the north it wrinkles into an endless line of large and small rolling hills. The lakes are 2 of the 194 in Kandiyohi County and lie at the southern end of the glacial lakes, in a geologic region known as the Leaf Hills.

This region measures 10 by 19 miles wide, extends 150 miles through west-central Minnesota, and contains some of the most unexpected scenery in Minnesota. Numerous glacial features have shaped the area into a landscape that will surprise you. The glacial debris left by the last ice age measures up to 450 feet deep in this region and formed Mount Tom, the highest point within 50 miles. Since my knowledge of this area came only from traveling through Willmar to the south, I left with a new

appreciation for this unique and beautiful region.

This ride begins in Kandiyohi County Park 7, a utilitarian name that belies the beauty of this park on the shore of Games Lake. From the park turn right onto CR 5. You'll enjoy the smooth pavement, ample shoulders, and excellent scenery of Sibley State Park as you cycle along this mostly flat road. As you continue along this road, it gracefully winds between Norway and Middle Lakes.

At 2.0 miles turn right onto CR 40, and notice that you've left the thick woods surrounding the lakes and now straddle the line between forest and farm. Compared with the small glacial hills you'll see later in this ride, the hills south of CR 40 are marked by longer and gentler grades. At 5.2 miles turn right onto CR 1, which takes you north toward the more scenic features left by the glaciers.

When you reach 8.9 miles, turn right onto Highway 9. Although this road isn't extremely busy, it is a state highway and carries more traffic than any of the others you'll ride during this loop. Fortunately, the highway has a paved shoulder for most of the half-mile you're on it, but it ends just before you turn left onto CR 1. Use caution when making this left turn.

After turning back onto CR 1, you'll face a short climb, choppy pavement, and the beginning of the best scenery of the ride. As you pedal through the countryside, you'll see endless hills in a countless variety of shapes and sizes, marshes formed from glacial kettles, and hilltop patches of prairie that alternate with forest and farm fields. This 8-mile section is the highlight of the ride because of its quiet roads and its landscape that never repeats itself. And though the surrounding fields and forest roll almost constantly, the road remains relatively flat, with only a couple of short climbs.

This region doesn't have the dramatic ravines and bluffs of the southeast, the omnipresent beauty of a moody Lake Superior, or an intricately carved valley like that of the St. Croix River, but it does provide a clear view of the true power of glaciers. At 17.6 miles you'll reenter the real world with a left

Ride 38: Norway and Games Lake Loop

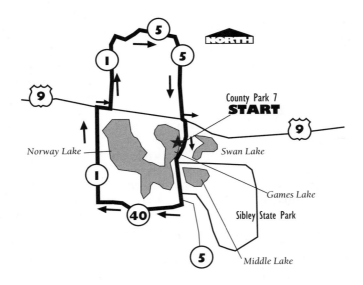

County Park 7
START

Norway Lake

Swan Lake

Games Lake

Sibley State Park

Middle Lake

Getting There

From New London go west on Highway 9 to CR 5. Go south on CR 5 to County Park 7.

DIREC-TIONS at a glance

0.0 Start at County Park 7 and turn right onto CR 5.
2.0 Turn right onto CR 40.
5.2 Turn right onto CR 1.
8.9 Turn right onto Highway 9.
9.4 Turn left onto CR 1.
13.1 Turn right onto CR 5.
17.6 Turn left onto Highway 9.
17.8 Turn right onto CR 5.
19.0 Return to park.

turn back onto Highway 9, followed thankfully by a right at 17.8 miles onto the smooth surface of CR 5. A few minutes later you'll reach the park, perhaps ready for a swim.

Prairie View Tour

Distance:	19.7 miles
Approximate Pedaling Time:	1.5 to 3 hours
Terrain:	Mostly flat, with a few gentle rolling hills
Traffic:	Light
Surface:	Smooth asphalt, with a couple of short stretches of choppy surface
Things to See:	Mix of farm fields and prairie, panoramic views to the west from CR 5, Camden State Park
Facilities:	Convenience store in Russell; camping, water, and restrooms in state park; numerous restaurants in Marshall

Besides being farm country, this part of southwestern Minnesota has another product that shows good potential for the local economy. For cyclists this product can make a flat ride feel hilly or a hilly ride feel flat. I'm referring to wind—and in this part of Minnesota, it blows often.

When you drive through the area around Marshall, you may notice some tall, futuristic looking towers with large propellers. What you're seeing are wind turbines that several companies have started using to generate electricity. Erected to take advantage of the winds that blow along the Buffalo Ridge, the tall structures have become a more common feature of the landscape during the past ten or so years.

The area is also home to Camden State Park, an oasis cut out of the surrounding prairie. Long ago the Redwood River sliced a

Ride 39: Prairie View Tour

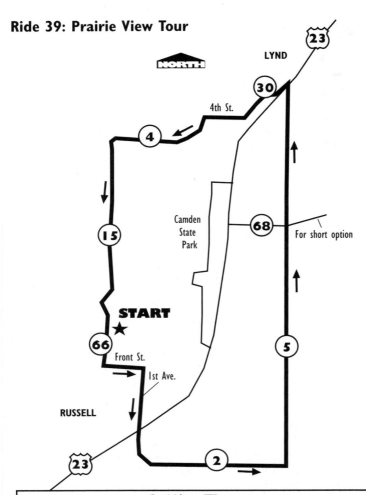

NORTH

LYND

23

30

4th St.

4

15

Camden State Park

68

For short option

START

★

66

Front St.

1st Ave.

5

RUSSELL

23

2

Getting There

From Marshall (which is 150 miles southwest of the Twin Cities), take Highway 23 south 14 miles to Russell; turn right on 1st Avenue, follow it 0.5 mile to Front Street, turn left onto Front; follow it to CR 66; and turn right and go 0.2 mile to the park.

DIREC-TIONS at a glance

0.0 Leave park and turn left onto CR 66.
0.2 Left onto Front Street.
0.3 Right onto 1st Avenue.
0.8 Cross Highway 23 and follow CR 2.
4.8 Left onto CR 5.
10.3 Left onto Highway 23.
10.6 Right onto CR 30 into Lynd.
11.1 Right onto 4th Street and follow it through town.
11.9 Left onto CR 4.
14.9 Left onto CR 15.
19.5 Left onto CR 66.
19.7 Arrive back at town park.

valley through the flat landscape, providing Indians and pioneers with food, shelter from the relentless prairie sun, free-flowing spring water, and protection from harsh winter winds. The river also contains brown trout, a rare sight in southwestern Minnesota. The predominant trees consist of maple, basswood, and ash, and numerous species of animals live in the sheltered valley.

Settlers arrived in the valley during the late 1840s and formed a small town, naming it after their home of Camden, New Jersey. The town grew until the railroad decided against building a depot there, and by the 1930s Camden was gone. The park lies on the Coteau des Prairie ("Highland of the Prairie"), a high plateau that rises as high as 900 feet above the land to the north and east. If you visit this area, don't expect to see an impressive butte rising from the prairie as you would see farther west, since the elevation change is nearly imperceptible.

The ride begins in the tiny town of Russell. After working

your way through town, cross Highway 23 and follow CR 2 for about 4 miles. You'll notice in this part of Minnesota that many of the county roads run straight for several miles at a time. With a mostly flat landscape and few valleys to negotiate, counties made the roads go as straight as possible.

At. 4.8 miles turn left onto CR 5. This road runs along a ridge that sits higher than much of the surrounding area. As you look west, you'll have sweeping, panoramic views of Lyon County. Although you probably didn't notice it on the previous road, you climbed ever so slightly to reach this point. Montana calls itself Big Sky Country, but gazing out over the prairie from this spine in the landscape proves that the Midwest also has plenty of big sky views.

At 10.3 miles turn left onto Highway 23 again and wind through the tiny town of Lynd. After a quick trip through the quiet village, turn left onto CR 4 at 11.9 miles for a short climb out of the shallow valley. Three miles later, at 14.9 miles, you'll turn left onto CR 15, where the landscape temporarily changes from fields of row crops to rolling pasture. After being lulled by thousands of acres of perfect green rows, you'll be startled to suddenly see grassy hills and fields. From CR 15 you'll see the tops of trees that sit in the valley of Camden State Park. Turn left on CR 66 at 19.5 miles for the short jaunt back to the park in Russell.

Camden State Park option

Instead of starting this loop in Russell, it's potentially much more interesting to ride from Camden State Park. The park makes an excellent origin for a variation of this loop, especially if you want to combine hiking or mountain biking with a road ride. From the park entrance cross Highway 23 to CR 68 and follow it for 2 miles, to CR 5. Turn left onto CR 5 and ride the loop as outlined above. To finish the ride, take CR 68 back to the park. This loop measures about 24 miles.

Chanarambie Valley Loop

Distance:	20.8 miles
Approximate Pedaling Time:	1.5 to 3 hours
Terrain:	Mostly flat, with gentle rolling hills and a 0.5 mile climb
Traffic:	Light
Surface:	Smooth asphalt
Things to See:	Beautiful little valley
Facilities:	No restaurants or lodging in Chandler; restaurants, historic district, shops, and national monument in Pipestone (25 miles west)

If you were driving on Highway 91 on your way to somewhere else, you'd pass Chandler and possibly not even remember seeing evidence of a town. This small village of a couple of hundred people barely registers as a dot on most maps. What most drivers don't see as they zip by is the serene Chanarambie Valley, which extends south of town. It's unlikely that most people will drive a long distance to ride this loop. But if you're passing through the area on I–90 (20 miles to the south) or visiting a nearby town, this ride is worth the stop.

Surrounded on all sides by large rolling fields of corn and soybeans, the gently sloped valley sides reminded me of a landscape from the West. Short prairie grass and the few cottonwoods scattered about help form a landscape that would fit perfectly in Montana. Instead, this small chunk of the high plains somehow ended up in the middle of southern Minnesota, hundreds of miles from where it should be.

From the middle of town, follow CR 4 west, staying left at

the split. For the next 6 miles you'll ride on new pavement along the flat valley floor. As you leave town, you may notice that virtually all the houses are new. A tornado nearly wiped out Chandler several years ago, and you're seeing a rebuilt town, not a new one that sprouted overnight with 1990s settlers. Just west of town a dead tree stands alongside the road, with a piece of sheet metal still wrapped around its lifeless branches, a somber reminder of the event.

If you've traveled through the western United States, you may feel as though you'd left Minnesota. At around 6 miles you'll climb the southern rim of the valley and enter the realm of southern Minnesota farmland. As you look west toward Pipestone, the slight ridge you're on provides a view that encompasses thousands of acres of farms stretching toward South Dakota.

At 8.3 miles you'll turn right onto CR 18, and follow it to CR 3, where, at 11.3 miles, you'll take another right. This road climbs gradually as it winds east along the edge of the valley. Although you can't see the main valley from this road, it does pass through one narrow branch of it—a gash in the fields marked by a large grove of mature trees. While most of the trees you'll see in this area surround farmhouses to serve as windbreaks, this may be a remnant of forests that once covered parts of southern Minnesota.

At 17.2 miles turn right to stay on CR 5. Enjoy the last 3 miles as the road continues to snake back to town. After a short descent back to the valley floor, turn right onto Highway 91 and follow it the short distance to your vehicle. To avoid riding on Highway 91, look for a paved residential street on your right before the hill and take that back to town.

Valley-only option

Riders who want a shorter trip or who don't want to climb out of the valley can ride CR 4 south from Chandler about 6 miles to the first climb. Turn around and return the same way for a 12-mile out-and-back trip.

Ride 40: Chanarambie Valley Loop

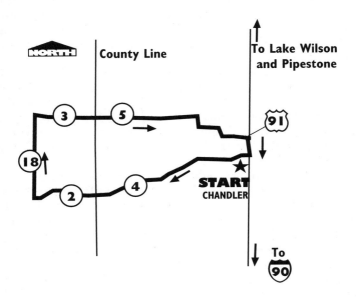

To Lake Wilson and Pipestone

To 90

Getting There

From Pipestone (which is 190 miles southwest of the Twin Cities), take Highway 30 east 18 miles to Highway 91, go south about 6 miles to Chandler, turn right into town, and park along Main Avenue.

DIREC-TIONS at a glance

0.0 Leave town on CR 4.
0.3 Stay left at split to stay on CR 4.
6.2 Road changes to CR 2 at county line.
8.3 Turn right onto CR 18.
11.3 Turn right onto CR 3.
13.8 Road changes to CR 5.
17.2 Turn right to stay on CR 5.
20.0 Turn right onto Highway 91.
20.8 Arrive back in town.

Appendix 1

Cycling Organizations

Minnesota Coalition of Bicyclists
P.O. Box 75452
St. Paul, MN 55175
(612) 452–9736 Hotline

Minnesota Office of Tourism
Metro Square
121 7th Place East
St. Paul, MN 55101
(612) 296–5029
(800) 657–3700
www.explore.state.mn.us

Mississippi Valley Women's
    Cycling Association
621 East 61st Street
Minneapolis, MN 55417
(612) 435–5734 Kathy

North Star Ski Touring Club
P.O. Box 4275
St. Paul, MN 55104
(612) 643–4453 Hotline

North Central Mountain
    Bike Group
1119 Kirkwood Drive
Eagan, MN 55123
(612) 452–0907
Gary Sjoquist

Paul Bunyan Cyclists
P.O. Box 2672
Brainerd, MN 56425
(218) 829–4206
Trail Blazers Bike Club
Suite 122–101 Parkdale Plaza
    Building
1600 South Highway 100
Minneapolis, MN 55416
(612) 541–0412

Twin City Bicycle Club
P.O. Box 131086
Roseville, MN 55113
(612) 924–2443 Hotline
This club schedules nearly 500
rides and trips per year around
Minnesota and the Twin Cities

Velo Duluth
1205 93rd Avenue West
Duluth, MN 55808
(218) 626–3574

Appendix 2

Bike Shops

Shops with an * rent bikes. If you need to rent, call ahead.

Adventure Cycle and Ski (Ride 1)
178 Center Street
Winona, MN 55987
(507) 452–4228

Bicycle Sports (Rides 3, 8, 9)
1409 South Broadway
Rochester, MN 55903
(507) 281–5007

The Bike Shop (Rides 29, 30, 31, 34, 35, 38)
612 Broadway
Alexandria, MN 56308
(320) 762–8493

The Bike Shop (Rides 36, 37, 39, 40)
219 West Main
Marshall, MN 56258
(507) 532–3633

Itasca Bike and Ski (Rides 19–20)
316 Northeast 4th Street
Grand Rapids, MN 55744
(218) 326–1716

Little River General Store (Ride 2) *
104 and 6 Parkway Avenue North
Lanesboro, MN 55949
(507) 467–2943

Outdoor Store (Rides 4–9)
323 Main Street
Red Wing, MN 55066
(612) 388–5358

Superior North Outdoor Center (Rides 22–23)
P.O. Box 177
Grand Marais, MN 55604
(218) 387–2186

Twin Ports Cyclery (Rides 21–22)
361 Canal Park Drive
Duluth, MN 55802
(218) 722–0106

Appendix 3

Minnesota Bike Rides

May

Clean Air Bike Festival
Apple Valley, MN (at Minnesota
    Zoo)
(612) 885–0338
8, 25, or 50 miles

Multiple Sclerosis 60–30 Bike Tour
Maplewood, MN (Twin Cities
    area)
(612) 870–1500
30 or 60 miles

Pedal DePonds Bike Tour
Fergus Falls, MN
(218) 739–4489 or 739–0125
50 or 100 kilometers, 18 or 100
    miles

Spring Tour
Avon, MN
(320) 363–1311
38 or 50 miles

Sykkle Tur
Preston, MN
(507) 467–2696
36 miles

Trek 100 Bike Ride
Twin Cities
(800) 248–8735
100 miles, 100 kilometers
    or 30 miles

June

Cal Miller Memorial Bike Ride
    and Race
Perham Chamber of Commerce
135 East Main Street
Perham, MN 56573
(800) 634–6112
12 to 36 miles

Heart of the Lakes Tour
Sauk Centre Chamber
    of Commerce
P.O. Box 222
Sauk Centre, MN 56378
(320) 352–5201
15, 35, or 60 miles

Riverfest Ride
Little Falls Chamber of Commerce
200 Northwest 1st Street
Little Falls, MN 56345
(320) 632–5155
56 miles

Tour of Lakes
Paul Bunyan Cyclists
P.O. Box 2672
Brainerd, MN 56425
(218) 829–4206
35 or 72 miles

July

Tour of Saints
P.O. Box 1996
Collegeville, MN 56321
(320) 363–1311
35 or 50 miles

August

Bike Tour for Cerebral Palsy
St. Cloud, MN
(320) 253–0765
10, 25, or 50 miles

Crow Wing Classic
Staples, MN
(218) 894–1515, ext. 334
25 or 50 miles

Duluth North Shore Tour
Velo Duluth
1205 93rd Avenue West
Duluth, MN 55808
(218) 626–3574
35, 50, 75, or 100 miles

Great River Ride
American Lung Association
4220 West Old Shakopee Road
  #101
Minneapolis, MN 55404
(612) 885–0338
40 to 70 miles per day (3 days)

A Midsummer Day's Ride
Northwest YMCA
3490 North Lexington Avenue
Shoreview, MN 55126
(612) 486–3808, ext 228
25 miles

September

Jesse James Bike Tour
P.O. Box 271
Northfield, MN 55057
(507) 645–3046
10, 30, 60, or 100 miles

St. Paul Classic Bike Tour
c/o NEC
475 North Cleveland Avenue #100
St. Paul, MN 55104
(612) 372–3424 Hotline
14 or 28 miles

October

Bike Ride Around Mille Lacs
Mille Lacs Health System
11234 Cove Drive
Onamia, MN 56359
(320) 532–3877
35 or 70 miles